THE PROOF OF HEAVEN & HELL

A Psychologist's journey to the Unknown Life

Dr. Robin K. Mathew

Writer's Pocket

First published by Writer's Pocket in 2025

email: editor@writerspocket.com

Cover Design by Dr. Robin K. Mathew

ISBN-13: 978-93-7248-672-8

www.writerspocket.com

To those whose pain was mistaken for imagination,

whose symptoms were written off as stories—

You were never the anomaly, never the error.

The world simply didn't know your name yet.

I dedicate this book to those who have endured the weight of misunderstood, misdiagnosed, and invisible medical conditions.

To the voices unheard and the pain unseen—your stories matter, and this is for you.

CONTENTS

Acknowledgements

The Proof of Heaven and Hell
A Psychologist's Journey into the Unknown life

This book was never a planned destination—it was a journey life quietly placed in my hands.
It was born not from ambition, but from years of witnessing suffering that often remains unnamed, unseen, and unheard.

I write this while still on my own path of healing. Yet every day I rise, because I have learned that purpose cannot wait when tomorrow is uncertain.

To everyone whose pain was dismissed, misunderstood, or unseen— to those told *"It's all in your head,"* when it lived in every silent struggle — you were never the error, never the anomaly.
The world simply had not learned your language yet.
This book is for you.

The insights within these pages are shaped by every voice I have heard—as a behavioural psychologist, researcher, ethnographer, and a lifelong student of the human mind. They carry the reflections of thousands of real stories, shared with trust and courage.

My deepest gratitude to the institutions that shaped my journey: **Centre for Addiction and Mental Health, University of Toronto; Athena Heilen Research Centre; University of Michigan; Thomson Reuters; Best Buy; University of Madras,** and all academic and non-academic spaces that taught me along the way.

My greatest thanks to my wife **Dr. Dhanya George**—my anchor and strength—who held me steady through my hardest days.

I am sincerely grateful to **Dr. Syam Krishnan**, Professor of Neurology at **Sree Chitra Tirunal Institute for Medical Sciences and Technology, Trivandrum**, for his support and endorsement of this work.

And to you, dear reader—thank you for opening these pages, for listening, and for allowing my words into your world. It is an honour to be read by you.

With gratitude,
Thank you.
Dr. Robin K Mathew

1

Proof of Heaven

There are stories—whispered across centuries—of people who claim to have died, crossed into another world, and returned. Doctors have recorded them. Philosophers have pondered them since the time of Aristotle. And though the voices come from different lands and ages, they speak of the same strange things: a radiant light, a heavenly realm, angels, ancestors, and the unmistakable presence of something divine.

Seeing God once, they say, can turn a soul to gold.

One of these voices belongs to Dr. Mary Neal, an American orthopedic spine surgeon—a woman of logic and science, not of superstition. She believed in facts, not miracles. But that changed one afternoon in 1999, on a wild river in Chile.

Mary and her husband were kayaking when the river turned violent. Their kayak flipped, trapping her beneath the surface. The current was merciless. Minutes passed. She struggled, then stopped struggling. The cold wrapped around her like a closing fist. She knew she was dying.

For thirty long minutes, her body lay still beneath the rushing water. When rescuers finally pulled her out, she wasn't breathing. By all measures, she was gone.

And yet—she came back.

Mary later said that in the instant her body gave up, something extraordinary began. From the dark water, she was drawn toward a soft, golden light. Around her stood beings she can only call angels—not the winged figures of paintings, but shapes of pure, overwhelming love. They didn't speak, yet she understood everything.

They led her to a place beyond words—a world of light and peace, where pain and fear no longer existed. There was only love.

But then, the angels told her something that filled her with sorrow. "Mary," they said, "your time has not yet come. You must go back. There is work still waiting for you."

She didn't want to return. The love she felt there was so vast, so perfect, that it made the world she'd left behind seem distant and cold. But they showed her flashes of her children's future—moments she was meant to witness—and gently sent her back.

Before she left, she heard a final message. God told her that her son would soon die in an accident.

Years later, that prophecy came true.

Mary wrote about her journey in *To Heaven and Back: A Doctor's Extraordinary Account of Her Death, Heaven, Angels, and Life Again.* And in her quiet, steady voice, she insists it was real. She says once you've touched heaven, the memory never fades. It changes everything.

Visiting mother in heaven

There are stories that sound like whispers from the edge of life—voices of those who died for a moment and came back with memories too vivid to forget.

One such voice is Ashley's.

She was young, full of life, when a road accident sent her into unconsciousness. For the doctors, she was just another critical patient in the intensive care unit. But Ashley later wrote something that still chills anyone who reads it:

"I could see my own body lying still in the hospital. I was wearing a blue gown, a mask covered my face, and machines surrounded me, humming softly. I wasn't inside my body anymore—I had left it. I was floating above it."

She described drifting upward, then entering a long, dark tunnel. It was silent—deep and endless—but she wasn't afraid. At the far end, a brilliant light was waiting. The closer she came to it, the calmer she felt, as though all the fear and pain she'd ever known were being washed away.

"I saw angels," she wrote, "their wings shimmering like pearls in that divine light. And then... I saw my mother. She had died two years before. She smiled at me. She was radiant. But she didn't speak. I just knew—I wasn't meant to stay. I had to go back."

Moments later, Ashley opened her eyes in the hospital bed. She was alive. But the world, she said, never looked the same again.

Stories like Ashley's aren't rare. Across time, people from every corner of the world have described the same mysterious crossing.

Anita Moorjani Hong Kong.

She was dying of cancer—her body frail, her consciousness slipping away. In those final hours, she says she saw a radiant halo of light, and within it, her deceased father. Around her was a feeling so vast and loving that she didn't want to return. But she did—and when she woke up, something impossible had happened. Her cancer was gone. Anita later told her story in Dying to Be Me: My Journey from Cancer, to Near Death, to True Healing, saying that love itself had healed her.

Centuries earlier, in 1740, a French doctor named Pierre Jean du Monchaux wrote the first recorded account of such an experience. In 1968, British researcher Celia Green gathered over four hundred testimonies from people who had left their bodies and returned.

Then came 1975—when American psychologist Raymond Moody gave these strange journeys a name. In his book *Life After Life*, he called them *Near-Death Experiences*. The stories he collected from a hundred people changed how the world thought about death.

Since then, thousands more have spoken. Different voices.

Different lives. Yet all describing the same light, the same peace, the same love that waits somewhere beyond the dark.

90 Minutes in Heaven

It was a cold morning on January 18, 1989, when Pastor Don Piper's car collided head-on with a truck on a Texas highway. The crash was brutal. When the paramedics arrived, there was nothing left to save. Don's heart had stopped. His body was still. His pulse was gone. He was pronounced dead at the scene.

But death, it seems, wasn't the end of his story.

For the next 90 minutes—while his body lay crushed and lifeless—Don Piper says he was somewhere else. Alive, aware, and surrounded by a light so pure it defied words.

"It was a place beyond description," he later said. "I was in a realm of peace and joy. I saw my loved ones who had passed—my great-grandmother among them. I heard music, not of this earth, sung by a choir that seemed to be made of light itself."

He spoke of colors that don't exist in this world, of warmth that felt like love made visible. Heaven, he said, wasn't a place of clouds and gates—it was a presence. Unity. Holiness. Joy beyond anything the human heart can contain.

And then, just as he began to explore that radiant world, something tugged at him. A sound—faint at first—grew stronger. Voices. People praying.

In an instant, he was back in his broken body, gasping for air. Against every medical explanation, Don Piper had returned to life.

The book *90 Minutes in Heaven: A True Story of Death & Life by Don Piper & Cecil Murphey* —is a story that continues to both comfort and puzzle us.

The Wonderfooled Boy

Years later, another story captured the world's attention. It was 2010 when a book titled *The Boy Who Came Back from Heaven* hit the shelves.

It told the story of Alex, a young boy who nearly died in a car accident with his father. The book described angels cradling his father, and one angel guiding Alex himself through heaven, where he claimed to have spoken with Jesus Christ.

The story spread like wildfire. Over a million copies were sold. People clung to it as proof that heaven was real.

But truth, as it often does, came quietly. Five years later, Alex sent a letter to the publishers. In it, he admitted the story wasn't true. His parents, he said, had pushed him to make it up. The visions, the angels, the meeting with Jesus—none of it had happened.

The book was pulled from publication. What began as a tale of faith had become a story of human frailty—the kind that reminds us how easily hope can be shaped, and sometimes misused.

Science of Near-Death Experiences

While some see these stories as proof of an afterlife, others turn to science for answers.

Dr. G. M. Woerlee, an anesthesiologist, explored these mysteries through a different lens in his book *Mortal Minds: The Biology of Near-Death Experiences.* He argues that such visions—the light, the tunnel, the feelings of peace—can be traced to the brain's final moments: the chemistry of oxygen loss, the flooding of endorphins, the mind's desperate effort to find meaning in its fading seconds.

The Strange Science of Seeing Yourself from outside

There's a word for this experience—heautoscopy. It means *to see oneself from outside.* Some call it the *doppelgänger effect*: a moment when you feel split in two—one body standing still, the other watching from afar.

There's even something darker—negative heautoscopy—when a person looks into a mirror and sees nothing at all. They feel hollow, as if their body has vanished.

Scientists trace these strange sensations to a small but powerful region of the brain called the temporoparietal junction. It's here that your mind pieces together signals from your senses to create a single, unified feeling of *being you.*

If this region is disturbed—even slightly—reality can slip. In laboratories, when doctors apply gentle electrical pulses to that part of the brain, volunteers report floating above themselves, watching their own bodies from the ceiling.

They swear they've left their flesh behind—when in truth, their brain has simply misfired.

Between Sleep and Death

Some people touch this same borderland while under anesthesia. They wake up mid-surgery, half-conscious, unable to move. Others report drifting outside their bodies just before sedation takes full hold.

Doctors say these sensations aren't signs of dying—but of the mind struggling to stay awake as chemicals pull it toward sleep.

The Oxygen Mirage

When oxygen levels in the blood fall—during cardiac arrest, drowning, or a fall from great height—the brain begins to fade. In those moments, vivid hallucinations bloom: lights, tunnels, angelic figures, the voices of loved ones.

It's the mind's final attempt to make sense of its own shutdown. When revived, people often describe these moments as journeys beyond death. But science sees them as the desperate, beautiful illusions of a starving brain.

The Body's Last Gift

Under extreme stress, the body releases endorphins—natural painkillers that fill the mind with peace, love, and even euphoria. It's nature's mercy, cushioning us from pain.

Combined with memories, beliefs, and expectations, these chemicals can paint an experience so radiant it feels like heaven itself.

The Chemical Gateways

Certain drugs, like ketamine, mimic this process. Used in anesthesia, it can pull people out of their bodies and into dreamlike realms of light and sound. Roughly one in a thousand patients experiences such visions when waking from surgery.

Even carbon dioxide—when it builds up in the blood—can twist perception. It can cause bright flashes, tunnels of light, and the strange feeling of moving toward something immense and luminous.

Between Science and the Soul

Perhaps these are all chemical illusions—mere sparks in the dying circuitry of the brain. Or perhaps, as some believe, they are doorways—a thin, trembling line between two worlds.

Science can describe the mechanisms. But it cannot explain the *feeling*. That moment when the body lies still, yet the self drifts upward—watching, waiting, wondering which side of life it truly belongs to.

Evidence and Experiences of "Heaven"

There are moments when science and mystery collide—when even those who study the brain find themselves questioning what lies beyond it.

Dr. Eben Alexander was one of them. A respected American neurosurgeon, trained to trust only what could be seen, measured, or cut open beneath a scalpel. But in 2008, his world changed.

He fell into a deep coma caused by a rare and devastating form of meningitis. His brain, by all medical accounts, had stopped functioning. For seven days, his body lay motionless, sustained only by machines.

And yet, when he woke, he spoke of another world.

Dr. Alexander said he had traveled through a place overflowing with light, color, and music—sounds that seemed to shimmer through the air. He was guided by a young woman with butterfly wings, her presence both familiar and otherworldly. She led him through landscapes that felt infinite, radiant with love.

Only later did he recognize her. She was his biological sister, whom he had never met—she had died years before he knew she existed.

He called his story *Proof of Heaven: A Neurosurgeon's Journey into the Afterlife.* And for many, it became exactly that—proof. A beacon of hope that there truly is something waiting beyond the veil of death.

But not everyone agreed.

Dr. Oliver Sacks, one of the world's leading neurologists, offered a quieter, sobering voice. He explained that near-death experiences are brief—lasting perhaps thirty seconds, a few minutes at most. Yet within that suspended moment, the mind stretches time, making it feel endless.

According to Dr. Sacks, what Dr. Alexander experienced likely occurred in the fragile space between coma and consciousness—when the brain, half-awake, begins to rebuild reality out of scattered fragments.

"The part of the brain that interprets experience can still fire during this transition," he said. "And when it does, dreams can take on the weight of truth."

It's easy, he added, to mistake the mind's final flickers for visions of heaven.

Perhaps that is why people who return from the edge often see what their hearts already believe: their own gods, their own loved ones, the symbols of their faith.

People who've come close to death often describe the same haunting sensation: leaving their bodies behind. Floating above the world, watching themselves from a distance, drifting toward a tunnel of light. To them, it feels real—more real than life itself. But what if the truth lies not beyond the body, but within the brain?

No one, after all, has ever returned claiming to have met forgotten gods from distant lands—or to have seen Abraham Lincoln deep in conversation with Emperor Louis XIV

Yet, despite all the explanations, the mystery remains.

Whatever these visions are—dreams, miracles, or memories from somewhere beyond—they remind us of one thing: When the body falls silent, the human mind still reaches for light.

2

Proof of Hell

Her hands were the first thing I noticed.

They trembled—not from cold, but from something unseen. Something that lived beneath the skin. Fear.

Eliser was a nurse. A gentle, steady soul who had left Morocco years ago to build a quiet life in Canada. She had no reason to be haunted—no tragedy, no shadow from her past. Her days were spent easing pain, closing the eyes of the dying, bringing calm to rooms filled with suffering. Twice, the hospital had honored her for her devotion.

And yet now, she couldn't hold a glass of water without spilling it.

When she finally spoke, her voice was a thin thread of sound. "I don't know what sin I've committed, Doctor," she said, her eyes flickering toward the wall as though something stood there, unseen. "But all I see now… is the devil."

Her words hung heavy in the air, like smoke after a fire.

"When I look at people," she continued, "their faces twist. Their eyes turn into black holes. Their skin looks burned. Their smiles—" she stopped, trembling— "their smiles stretch too wide. And when I look in the mirror, I see horns on my own head."

She wasn't lost to madness. She knew exactly where she was. She could tell you the color of the curtains, the hum of the air vent, the way my pen tapped against the table.

Everything around her was clear. It was only faces that had turned into monsters.

She was trapped in a waking nightmare of flesh. I had read about this once, buried in a medical journal—a rare condition called

prosopometamorphopsia, or **PMO**. It's not madness. It's not possession. It's a fault line in the brain's face-recognition system, where sight and meaning get tangled.

For someone with PMO, the world remains normal—until a face appears. Then, something inside the visual cortex misfires. Eyes sink into pits. Skin warps. Mouths twist. The mind knows it's seeing a person, but the face becomes a mask of horror.

The cause is usually damage near the **fusiform gyrus**, a small region that helps us recognize faces. A tumor, a stroke, a tiny bleed—it doesn't take much to shatter that delicate map.

For Eliser, that fault line had opened wide.

Her husband's familiar smile now looked like something from a nightmare. Her own reflection terrified her. And in her quiet moments, when logic faded, she wondered if she was cursed—if some restless spirit had followed her home from the ward.

But the truth wasn't in any spirit. It was in her brain.

A scan revealed a **meningioma**—a benign tumor, pressing against the part of her brain that helped her recognize faces. It wasn't evil. It wasn't punishment. It was pressure—simple, physical, devastating pressure.

"This isn't hell," the neurosurgeon told her gently. "It's your brain trying to make sense of broken signals. And we can fix it."

The surgery was delicate. Hours passed. When she awoke, she was exhausted but calm. Two days later, we handed her a mirror.

She hesitated. Then slowly, she lifted it. Her breath caught. Her reflection—clear, human, whole—stared back. No fangs. No hollow eyes. No horns.

She laughed—a trembling, astonished laugh that filled the room with light.

The devils had vanished.

Eliser's story wasn't about sin or punishment. It was about how fragile vision—and sanity—can be. How a small lesion can turn love into terror, a face into a monster. But it was also about recovery—how light, once lost, can return.

"The scariest demons are the ones the mind paints with its own hands."

3

The Devils Within

Some hauntings don't come from ghosts. They come from the mind itself—when sight falters, when sleep is stolen, when the brain begins to dream while awake.

a. The Visions of Father René

It began quietly, almost gently—just a blur in the margins of holy words.
Father René, a priest well into his seventies, noticed the lines in his Bible begin to drift, the letters softening as though they were sinking into water. He blamed the dim chapel lamps, the fatigue of age, or perhaps the long hours he spent bent in prayer.

But soon, the world around him began to shimmer with something he could not explain. It started with color—tiny bursts at the corners of his eyes, glimmering like gems in candlelight. Then came shapes. People. Animals. Things that did not belong in his quiet stone church.

He saw little men in red coats marching neatly along the altar rail. A white horse stood beside the confessional, still as a statue—except for its eyes, which were too many. The visions made no sound. They simply looked back at him, calm, unblinking, unreal.

Father René feared his mind was unraveling.
He prayed harder, fasted longer, searched his soul for hidden sins. But the visions stayed, faithful as shadows.

When he finally spoke to his doctor, she listened without surprise. Her voice was gentle, almost tender.
"What you see," she said, "has a name. It's called Charles Bonnet Syndrome."

She explained that when the eyes grow weak, the brain—unwilling to surrender to darkness—begins to create its own light. It paints pictures in the emptiness, filling the silence left by sight. There was no madness in him, only the loneliness of fading vision. With new lenses and brighter lamps, the phantoms began to retreat. The white horse faded first. Then the tiny soldiers dissolved into air.

One morning, while reading his Bible bathed in sunlight, Father René realized they were gone. The chapel was still once more.

Yet sometimes, when the evening deepens and the candles tremble low, he feels a flicker at the edge of his vision—as if the lost visitors wait there still, quiet and patient, just beyond the light.

b. The Fire Inside

It began one night in a cramped apartment above a bar—a man named Thomas, trying to quit drinking alone.
For years, whiskey had been his silence, his comfort, his prayer. When he finally decided to stop, he expected pain—a dry mouth, a pounding head, maybe trembling hands. But what came for him was far darker.

Two days after his last drink, the world began to twist. The walls moved, slow and liquid, like they were breathing. Shadows crawled across the ceiling—first like insects, then birds, then faces that melted before he could name them. Heat surged beneath his skin, though the room was cold. His heart pounded against his ribs, desperate to escape something that wasn't there.

He tried to pray, but the words slipped through his mind like water. His hands shook so violently that the glass he reached for shattered on the floor.
When his brother found him hours later, Thomas was soaked in sweat, trembling, whispering about fire and wings and eyes in the dark.

At the hospital, the doctor's voice was calm, almost kind. "You're not losing your mind," she said. "Your body is just remembering what it can't have."

What Thomas was facing had a name—Delirium Tremens.
A severe reaction to sudden alcohol withdrawal.
When the brain loses the numbing touch of alcohol, it turns restless, electric. The nerves misfire. The body burns from the inside. Confusion, fever, shaking, visions so real they eclipse reason—this was not madness, but the brain's rebellion.

With treatment—fluids, sedatives, quiet care—the storm began to fade. By the third day, the walls stood still.
The crawling shadows vanished. Only silence remained—thick, heavy, and merciful.

Later, when he could finally speak, Thomas said softly, "It wasn't the fear that broke me. It was how real it all felt. Like my mind was on fire… and I couldn't tell what was burning."

c. The Burning Cities

His name was Daniel. Twenty-four years old. Soft-spoken, thoughtful, and once a brilliant art student. He used to paint quiet things — empty train stations, rain on windows, faces half-hidden in shadow. But then, the paintings began to change.

It started with whispers — faint, like someone calling from the next room. Then came the feeling of being watched. The shadows in the corners grew sharper, closer. One night, Daniel stayed awake until dawn, staring at the walls, convinced something was crawling just beneath the paint.

Over the weeks that followed, he transformed his room into a burning landscape. Whole cities painted in red and black flames stretched across every wall. When his mother asked what he was painting, he only said, "They're coming."

To Daniel, the warnings were real. The voices in the radio static told him things no one else could hear. The eyes behind the mirror blinked when he looked away. He believed the world was about to end — and only he could see it happening.

When his family brought him to the hospital, the doctors didn't speak of demons or spirits. They spoke of **schizoaffective disorder** — a mental illness where symptoms of schizophrenia and mood disturbance intertwine. His brain, they explained, was sending false signals, blending emotion and imagination until fear became vision.

Through medication, therapy, and time, the cities on fire began to cool. The voices softened. He still paints — but now his work holds both darkness and light, as if he's learned to live with what his mind once tried to destroy.

When asked what it felt like, Daniel paused for a long time and said, "It's like being awake inside a dream that doesn't want to end."

d. The Voices in the Quiet

It happened to Elena, a 34-year-old mountaineer trapped in her cabin during a brutal snowstorm in the Alps. The radio was dead, the road buried, and the nearest village a day's walk away. For the first few days, she kept busy — melting snow for water, rationing food, writing in her journal by lantern light.

But by the sixth night, the silence had changed. It wasn't peaceful anymore. It felt *alive.*

At first, she heard faint footsteps outside — crunching softly in the snow. When she opened the door, there was nothing. Then came the whispering — gentle, like someone talking just behind her shoulder. She turned again and again, but no one was there.

By the second week, the loneliness began to hum in her bones. One evening, as she sat near the dying fire, a man appeared in the corner of the room — tall, familiar somehow, with a kind expression. He spoke to her softly, telling her stories from her childhood, things only she could know. She wept with relief.

When rescue teams finally reached her days later, she asked where the man had gone — the one who had kept her company through the storm. They looked at her strangely. No footprints. No second bedroll. Just Elena, alone in the snow.

Doctors later told her it was isolation hallucination, a common experience among people who endure long stretches of solitude. When deprived of human contact, the brain begins to create its own company — voices, faces, even entire people — to protect itself from the crushing weight of loneliness.

Elena recovered, but she said part of her missed the man who wasn't real. "He was kind," she said quietly. "Kinder than the silence.

William James once wrote, "The world we think is solid is only a thin illusion floating on a sea of mystery."

And he was right. Because the line between heaven, hell, and the human brain is thinner than a breath. Sometimes the monsters people see are not born of darkness.

They're born of light—of neurons misfiring, of the mind trying desperately to make sense of the impossible.

4

The Holy-Smoke Seizure

Keshav was a tall, quiet young man from Gujarat—gentle in manner, his voice barely rising above a whisper. Though he now lived with his parents in a Western country, the traces of his roots clung to him: sacred threads tied around his wrist, a thin streak of ash on his forehead, a small temple pendant glinting softly against his chest.

When his parents walked into my office, their faces carried a strange glow—part pride, part unease. They sat down before me, the air thick with incense that seemed to follow them from the temple.

Before I could even ask a question, his mother leaned forward, her bangles chiming faintly.

"Doctor," she began with unshakable conviction, "our son is blessed. The goddess enters his body when he prays. We have seen it with our own eyes many times."

Her husband nodded, eyes lowered in reverence.

Between them, Keshav sat silent — his body tense, his gaze fixed on the floor. I asked gently, "Can you tell me what happens when the goddess comes?"

His mother's eyes brightened. "He shakes, he falls, his eyes turn upward. It is not sickness, Doctor — it is divinity. We are lucky to have such a son."

But Keshav's expression said otherwise. His hands gripped the chair like he was holding himself together. I asked his parents to wait outside. When the door closed, the room fell quiet — the kind of quiet that feels heavy, like it might break if anyone breathed too hard.

He spoke finally, his words barely a whisper.

"Doctor… I don't believe in any of this."

He looked exhausted, like he'd been carrying that sentence for years. "Every time I go to the temple," he said, "I smell it before we even reach the gate — the camphor, the smoke, the saffron. Then my head starts spinning. My throat tightens. My hands tremble. And before I know it, I'm on the ground. My body moves on its own. I can't stop it."

He swallowed hard. "And everyone around me starts praying. They think the goddess has entered me. But I'm just trying to breathe. I want to scream for help, but I can't."

His voice cracked, but he went on. "The priest told my parents I'm blessed. But I feel cursed, Doctor."

I leaned closer, choosing my words carefully.
"Keshav… this isn't a curse. It isn't a goddess either. What's happening to you is a kind of seizure. It's not your soul — it's your brain reacting to certain smells. The smoke you breathe triggers a reaction deep inside your head. It's real, it's medical — and it can be treated."

He looked up, startled, as if the idea of being human again was harder to believe than being divine.
"So… I'm not possessed?"

I smiled softly. "No, Keshav. You're not possessed. You're not broken. You're having what doctors call a Temporal lobe seizure — sometimes called the 'holy-smoke seizure' because it's triggered by strong smells like incense or camphor. It's your brain's misfire, not a spirit."

He stared at me for a long moment, trying to let that truth sink in.

The Science of Divinity

These events belong to a group of seizures called **focal aware seizures** — once known as simple partial seizures. They begin in the **temporal lobe**, where memories, emotions, and smells intertwine.

During these moments, the person stays awake and aware but feels trapped inside strange sensations:

- They might smell something burning — rubber, smoke, incense — even when nothing's there.
- They may taste something bitter or metallic.
- Some feel a wave of déjà vu or a sudden surge of emotion — fear, bliss, or sorrow.

It lasts only seconds or minutes. Then, as suddenly as it began, it ends — leaving behind confusion, exhaustion, and shame.

The cause? A spark of abnormal electrical activity near the **olfactory cortex** — the brain's smell center. The scent isn't imagined. It's created from within.

Keshav's seizures were triggered by the very smoke meant to bring peace. The temple that promised him salvation had unknowingly become the place that stole his breath.

With a neurologist's help, we built him a plan. Medication. Avoiding heavy incense. Learning to sense the warning signs before the storm.

Months later, he returned. The red thread still circled his wrist, the pendant still rested against his heart — but something had changed.

He smiled, small but steady. "Doctor," he said quietly, "I don't faint anymore."

The room seemed brighter then. His silence no longer trembled with fear. It rested — calm, grounded, whole. Outside, the city buzzed with its usual chaos. Inside, Keshav's stillness felt like peace.

"The line between miracle and medicine is thinner than smoke — and just as easy to breathe in."

5

She Laughs and Goes Blind

The first time I met Nadia, she entered my office clutching her mother's hand. She was twelve — thin, shy, with two perfect braids and a little yellow notebook covered in stickers. Her eyes were curious, but her smile… that was something she held back, as if even happiness might hurt her.

Her mother sat down beside her, her voice trembling. "She's afraid to laugh," she said softly.

Nadia kept her gaze fixed on the floor, twisting the edge of her T-shirt between her fingers.

I leaned forward. "Tell me what happens, Nadia."

For a moment, she didn't speak. Then, in a whisper, she said, "When I laugh… everything disappears. It's like someone turns off the lights inside my head. I can't see anything. And my head starts shaking… like it's not mine anymore."

Her mother added quickly, "It only lasts half a minute. But she panics. She won't play with her friends. She tries not to laugh at all."

The thought of a child avoiding laughter — her most natural joy — felt unbearably wrong.

We ran the tests: **MRI, EEG, CT** — the usual search for hidden storms. Each result told the same quiet truth.
Nadia's blindness wasn't imagined. It was real — caused by a tiny electrical surge deep inside her brain.

Whenever she laughed, the joy itself lit up the wrong circuit — a burst of energy firing through her **occipital lobe**, the part that lets us see. For a few seconds, that surge overloaded her vision.

Then the world went dark.

The condition had a strange name: **gelastic epilepsy** — "gelastic," from the Greek word GELOS, meaning laughter.

In Nadia's case, the laughter wasn't fake or forced — it was real joy triggering a real storm.
And hidden behind it all was a small, noncancerous mass in her brain — a **hypothalamic hamartoma**.
Tiny. Silent. Sending out rogue signals whenever emotions rose too high.

When I showed her mother the scans, the room fell quiet. Then I turned to Nadia. "This isn't your fault," I said. "Your brain is just sending the wrong signals. But we can help it learn to be still again."

She looked up, her eyes wide and wet. "Will I ever be able to laugh?"

"Yes," I said. "You'll laugh again. And next time, the world will stay bright."

Treatment began — medication to steady the misfiring signals in her brain. Surgery would only come if nothing else worked. For now, we waited, carefully, patiently.

Weeks turned into months. Then one morning, Nadia returned, wearing a bright red jacket and the kind of smile that had been missing for too long.

"I laughed at a joke in class," she said, her voice trembling between disbelief and joy. "And this time… I could still see."

It wasn't a cure. Not yet. But it was enough.

For the first time in years, she wasn't afraid of happiness. The world had stayed lit — even when she laughed.

"Laughter and light are born from the same place in the brain. Sometimes, fixing one helps the other find its way home."

6

The Flashlight of God

This story comes from a quiet corner of Australia — the kind of place where the land hums after rain, and the sky feels close enough to touch. Doctors still whisper about it, even now — half in awe, half in disbelief. It's the story of a man named Mark. Some even consider it as an urban myth.

Mark was forty-two, a quiet man who carried storms inside him. For years, his life had been ruled by **temporal lobe epilepsy** — seizures that came without warning, stealing moments from his days and sleep from his nights.

Medication helped, but never fully.
Every sunrise began with the same question: Will it happen again today? One afternoon, the world was calm. Mark stood by a river, fishing rod in hand, the water moving slow and silver beneath a darkening sky. The air smelled of wet earth and iron.

Then came the flash. A white blaze split the sky, brighter than anything human eyes were made to bear. The thunder hit almost at the same instant — a sound that seemed to tear the air apart. A tree just meters away exploded into fire.

Mark never even saw it. He dropped where he stood, body seizing once, then falling still.

When the paramedics reached him, there was no pulse. No breath. His heart had stopped for **some minutes**, he lay between two worlds — silent, unbreathing, eyes open to the storm above.

And then — a spark. A twitch beneath the ribs. A heartbeat. Mark came back. In the hospital, his wife Andrea held him as if he might slip away again.

"You were gone," she whispered.

Mark met her eyes, weak but certain.

"I didn't leave," he said quietly. "Not really."

The miracle wasn't that he survived the lightning.

It was what came after. Days turned to weeks. Weeks into months. A year passed. Eighteen years later, they still have not returned. The seizures — the ones that had haunted him for decades — were gone. Completely.

Mark drives. He works. He laughs easily now. Sometimes he goes back to that same river, casts his line, and watches sunlight ripple across the water.

"That lightning didn't kill me," he says. "It cured me. God touched me through the storm."

What Science Found

Doctors ran every test they could. His brain scans showed something extraordinary — a small **scar inside the hippocampus**, deep in the temporal lobe. It was the same place his seizures had always begun.

The lightning, they realized, had done what years of medication could not. It had **burned out the seizure focus** — almost exactly like a surgeon's laser ablation, the modern procedure used to cure certain types of epilepsy.

Only this time, nature — or fate — had done it by accident.

His neurologist later said softly, "You can call it divine. You can call it physics. But something passed through that man — something both fierce and merciful."

Medically, what happened wasn't a "spontaneous recovery." In neurology, that term means seizures simply fade on their own, without cause. Mark's case was different. The lightning acted like an **unintended ablation**, destroying a tiny cluster of overactive brain cells that had caused his epilepsy all along. In other words — the storm that nearly killed him, healed him instead. This anectodal evidence still remains a mystery.

"Maybe miracles are just science we haven't learned to name yet."

7
The Vision of Heaven

His name was Samuel — a preacher whose voice could fill a church with both thunder and tenderness. Faith lived in his every word, every gesture. But on the day he came to see me, there was something different in his eyes — There was a tremor in his hands, a strange shimmer in his eyes — the look of a man who'd glimpsed something too bright to hold.

"Doctor," he said, his voice shaking, "I saw God. I saw three halos around the sun. It was a revelation — clear as day."

I leaned forward. "Tell me what happened." He drew a long breath, his eyes far away.

"It was summer," he said softly. "The air was so hot it shimmered. I'd stepped outside to pray. The sky was cloudless — only light, endless light. Then I looked up…"

He stopped. For a moment, silence. Then his voice dropped to a whisper.

"The sun wasn't alone. Around it were three perfect rings of fire. Colors moved through them — gold, violet, red — like living flames. I fell to my knees. I thought, 'This is God showing Himself.' I've spoken of faith my whole life, but that day… I felt it touch me."

To **Samuel**, it was a vision. To medicine, it was something else. When he finished speaking, the room seemed to hold its breath. Then I said quietly, "Samuel, what you saw wasn't from the sky. It was from inside you — from your brain."

He looked startled. "My brain?"

"Yes," I said gently. "The part of your brain that lets you see — the **occipital lobe** — had a surge of activity. It's called a **visual aura**. Sometimes it happens before a migraine, sometimes before a seizure. Those halos, that light — they weren't in the heavens. They were created by your mind."

He stared at the floor, his voice barely a whisper. "So… it wasn't God?"

I shook my head slowly. "What you felt was real. The vision, the awe — all of it. But it was your brain's own lightning. A moment where electricity painted your faith in color."

He was quiet for a long time. Then he said, "But it felt more real than anything I've ever known."

And that, I told him, was the strangest part of all. The human brain can make light feel like divinity. It can turn a simple burst of neurons into something that shakes the soul.

Throughout history, people have seen halos in the sky, faces in clouds, angels in the glow of the sun — not realizing that sometimes, those visions bloom from within us.

Weeks later, Samuel came back. The visions were gone. His headaches had eased. But there was still a softness in his eyes — a quiet peace that hadn't been there before.

"It was beautiful," he said, almost to himself. "And frightening."

"Yes," I said. "That beauty had a name — migraine aura. Not heaven opening up, but your brain calling out."

He smiled faintly, looking out the window at the afternoon light. "Maybe both," he said. "Maybe God just used my brain as His canvas."

"The mind is a cathedral. Sometimes, when the doors open, even reason must kneel."

8

When the Blind See Clear Visions

Nirmal Jain. Seventy-nine years old. A woman made of kindness — the kind that stays soft even after the world turns hard.

She had once walked from village to village with a quiet smile and a shawl over her shoulder, helping whoever crossed her path. But now, her world was shrinking.

Her sight was fading — not all at once, but gently, cruelly — as if the light itself was slipping away one grain at a time. Faces blurred. Words disappeared. The world became a painting slowly dissolving into fog. Her doctor had called it macular degeneration.

One afternoon, as the sun dipped low and the kettle hissed softly beside her, something strange happened.

A little girl appeared by the window. She wore a red coat, her smile gentle, her eyes shining as if lit from within. Nirmal blinked, startled — and the girl was still there.

She didn't speak. She only stood in the light, quiet and calm, like a memory that had come home.

The next morning, it was monks — tall figures in saffron robes, walking silently across her living room floor. Their garments rippled in a breeze that didn't exist.

Then came others. Ancient temples glowing in the corner of her eye. Gardens blooming with impossible color. Faces of strangers that somehow felt familiar.

One night, her voice trembled as she told her daughter, "I see people who aren't alive anymore. I think… they've come for me."

Her daughter froze — half fear, half heartbreak. The next morning, she brought her to see me.

When they entered my office, Nirmal looked almost ashamed, her hands folded in her lap. I listened quietly as she spoke. When she finished, I said softly, "Nirmal… you're not losing your mind. What you're seeing is real — but it's not coming from outside. It's coming from your brain."

She frowned slightly. "From my brain?"

"Yes," I said. "It's called Charles Bonnet Syndrome. When people lose part of their sight, their brain doesn't stay silent. It begins to fill in the gaps with its own images — faces, shapes, even whole scenes. It's like your mind is painting what your eyes can no longer see."

Her eyes widened, a single tear gathering in the corner. "So… I'm not dying?"

I smiled. "No, Nirmal. You're not dying. You're witnessing your mind's art — your brain's way of refusing to live in darkness."

After that day, she stopped fearing her visions.

The little girl in red still came to the window. The monks still crossed the room at dusk. But now, Nirmal greeted them with a soft nod, as one might greet old friends.

In a world where her eyes had gone dim, her brain had lit a lantern of its own — painting beauty on the walls of her fading sight.

She was not haunted. She was blessed by the strange mercy of the mind — a light that continues to burn even when the world grows dark.

"When the body forgets, the brain remembers. When the eyes close, the mind begins to see."

9

Sounds that Kill You

Let me tell you about a girl named Ananya. She was thirteen—bright-eyed, curious, the kind of girl whose laughter could light up a room. But behind that laughter lived something unseen, something that waited quietly inside the most ordinary sounds.

It began with silence. Then came the betrayal of tiny noises—the faint crackle of a biscuit wrapper, the soft chewing of gum, the rhythmic tap of a pencil.

To most people, they were nothing. Everyday sounds. But to Ananya, they were unbearable. Each sound struck her like a sudden flame, sharp and impossible to escape.

"It doesn't just bother me," she whispered once. "It feels like my whole body is burning. I want to scream. I want to run. I can't breathe."

One morning, her teacher walked in wearing new shoes that squeaked with every step. That was all it took. Ananya's heartbeat went wild, pounding against her ribs. The sound sliced through her like glass. In seconds, she was running out of the classroom, tears smudging her vision.

Later, she said softly, *"I know it sounds crazy. But I'd rather vanish than hear it again."*

That day, her teacher didn't see disobedience—she saw fear. And that was where understanding began.

There was a name for the thing that haunted her. Misophonia. Often called *"selective sound sensitivity syndrome,"* Misophonia is a neurological disorder where certain everyday sounds trigger intense emotional and physical reactions—anger, disgust, panic, or overwhelming anxiety. The sounds that trigger it are often quiet and subtle—chewing, breathing, tapping, the click of a pen or the hum of typing fingers.

For someone like Ananya, the reaction isn't a matter of irritation—it's instant and uncontrollable. Her body tenses, her heart races, her hands tremble. It's as if her brain mistakes harmless sounds for danger.
The amygdala—the alarm center of the brain—doesn't whisper. It screams.

Researchers believe this happens because of an over connection between the brain's hearing system and the emotional centers, particularly a region called the anterior insular cortex (AIC). The AIC processes feelings like disgust and bodily awareness. In misophonia, it goes into overdrive at the slightest trigger, flooding the body with distress signals.

The result? Everyday life becomes a minefield. A family meal, a quiet classroom, even a friend's breathing can turn unbearable. Many who suffer from it avoid such situations entirely, leading to loneliness, anxiety, and a constant sense of being misunderstood. And yet, Misophonia isn't the same as *Hyperacusis*, where loudness itself causes pain. Here, it's not the volume that hurts—it's the *pattern*, the *source*, the very *presence* of certain sounds that feels like an attack.

When we explained all this to Ananya's parents, we said gently, "She isn't being stubborn. Her brain is wired to panic."

There was no cure—but there was light. Soft music to drown the harshest sounds. Therapy to teach her mind to slow down when the storm began. And above all, patience.

Her classmates stopped teasing. Her teacher moved her seat by the window. Her parents began to listen—to her words, and to her silences.

And slowly, Ananya began to return.

"The sounds are still there," she said one afternoon, her voice calm, "but now they don't own me."

Misophonia hides in the hum of the everyday. But once you name it—and meet it with understanding—it begins to lose its claws.

"Sometimes, the quietest battles are the loudest ones inside your head."

10

When Water knocks you out

There are the familiar reasons a person might fall into a seizure—flashing lights, sleepless nights, sudden stress. Doctors know those stories well.

But once in a while, medicine meets something so strange, it feels less like science and more like a haunting. This one began with a boy who feared not darkness, nor thunder, but water.

He was nine—playful, curious, always running barefoot through the lanes after the monsoon rain. In India, where the rivers are wide and the sky opens without warning, he loved to splash in puddles, swim in the local stream, and chase raindrops. Nothing ever happened then.

Until the evening bath.

Every night, when his mother poured water gently over his head, something inside him changed. The moment the first stream touched his scalp, his small body went rigid. His eyes rolled upward, hands began to tremble. Within seconds, it was over. He blinked, confused, as if waking from a dream he couldn't remember.

"It's like the water attacks him," his mother whispered. "We're afraid to bathe our own child."

Doctors doubted it at first—water couldn't possibly cause a seizure. But when they saw it for themselves, their disbelief dissolved.

They placed electrodes across his head, the EEG humming softly beside him. Then, with careful hands, the nurse poured a thin stream of water over his hair.

The screen erupted in a storm of light. The temporal lobe—the region of emotion, memory, and fear—flared with violent energy. The boy's brain was misfiring, treating falling water like an alarm bell. Yet scans showed no injury, no infection, no tumor.

There was only a name: Water-Immersion Epilepsy.

A ghostly reflex that appears in fewer than one in ten thousand people with epilepsy. Also known as Primary Bathing Epilepsy, it is one of the rarest forms of *reflex epilepsy*—where seizures are triggered not by chance, but by a specific, consistent stimulus. In this case, the simple touch of water.

For some, the temperature matters—cold water can provoke it more strongly. For others, even a few drops on the skin can awaken the storm. The seizures usually begin in one part of the brain (focal seizures) but can spread, seizing control of the body entirely. Many describe a strange warning beforehand—a flicker of dizziness, a sudden fear, a feeling like the world is tilting.

Doctors believe the cause lies in the brain's sensory wiring. When water touches the skin, it sends a flood of signals to the brain—tactile, thermal, rhythmic. In most people, these signals blend into the calm sensation of bathing. But in the boy's brain, the flood became chaos. The sensory centers overloaded, and the electrical rhythm of the mind collapsed into seizure.

This rare condition carries its own silent danger—the risk of drowning. So every bath became an act of caution, every drop of water measured with care.

The family learned to live softly around it. They washed him with cloths, avoided pouring water directly on his head, and used medicine to steady his mind. Slowly, the fear loosened. The water that once betrayed him became something gentler again.

What had begun as terror ended with understanding. Because sometimes, even in the strangest corners of medicine, fear gives way to peace.

11

The Girl who Undresses in Public

Most people think they know what epilepsy looks like — a body collapsing, limbs jerking, foam at the mouth. But epilepsy wears many faces. Some of them are quiet. Some are strange enough to break your heart.

This story is about a girl named Shari. Sixteen. Soft-spoken. Kind eyes. The kind of girl who smiled even when she was tired. And then one day, her body began to tell a story her mind didn't know.

There was no cry, no fall, no trembling fit. Just a moment — and she would start unbuttoning her shirt, pulling at her clothes as if something inside her demanded it. She would stand exposed, trembling and dazed, her eyes empty of awareness. When the moment passed, she'd wake to a wall of stares — strangers frozen, her mother rushing forward, covering her with a shawl, tears burning her cheeks.

At first, people whispered. They said she was seeking attention. That she was possessed. That she had no shame. Her mother tried everything — prayers, rituals, holy water, all the words meant to drive out invisible evil. But nothing worked.

By the time they reached the doctor, the family had already been worn down by judgment and fear. The doctor listened. He didn't flinch or frown. He only said, softly, "This is not her fault."

He explained that during certain seizures — especially in the **temporal lobe**, the part of the brain that governs emotion and self-control — something short-circuits. The person can move, act, even speak, but they're not truly there. It's called **ictal disrobing** — "ictal" meaning during a seizure, "disrobing" meaning exactly what it sounds like.

Shari wasn't choosing this. She wasn't aware. Her brain was momentarily hijacked by its own storm.

When her mother heard that, she didn't speak for a while. She just wept — not from despair, but from the relief that comes when a curse finally has a name.

With the right medication and care, the storms grew fewer. Shari began to live again, not as a mystery or a scandal, but as a girl with an illness — one that could be treated, one that didn't define her.

Her story remains rare, but it carries a truth most people forget: The hardest part of illness isn't always the illness itself. It's being misunderstood by the world.

12

When Music Creates Seizures

Most of us carry songs like memories — tucked somewhere deep, ready to bring back the scent of rain, a childhood laugh, or a face long gone. Music heals, lifts, softens. But for one young woman, it did something else entirely.

Her name was Cathy. Twenty-three years old. She lived in a quiet English town where church bells marked the hours and the air smelled faintly of damp earth. She loved music. She always had. Until the day a song — a simple hymn from her childhood — began to turn against her.

It started with a few notes. Just a melody she knew by heart. And then, suddenly, her heart would begin to pound. Her body would go rigid. She said it felt as if something inside her head was being pulled, hard — like invisible hands tugging at the threads of her mind. Then everything would go black.

When she woke, there would be faces around her, worried, whispering. And always, the same question: What happened?

"Doctor," she told him softly, "it's not every song. Just that one. A few lines, and I feel it coming." Her voice trembled. "It's like the music reaches somewhere it shouldn't."

The doctors ran their tests. Her scans were clear — no tumor, no damage, nothing out of place. But when they placed electrodes on her scalp and played that one song, the truth appeared in flashing waves across the screen.

The right temporal lobe — the part of the brain that holds emotion, sound, and memory — burst into electric chaos. The hymn wasn't just a tune. It was a trigger. Her brain didn't just hear the music —

it felt it too deeply, too powerfully, until feeling itself became dangerous.

"Cathy," the doctor said gently, "this isn't your fault. Your brain reacts to music the way others might react to pain or fear. The emotion is too strong — and it becomes a storm."

They called it **musicogenic epilepsy** — seizures born from sound. A rare and quiet condition, so unusual that most doctors never see a case in their lifetime.

With care, medicine, and time, the storms grew weaker. Cathy learned to listen carefully to her own silence — to know which songs to avoid, which memories to keep at a distance. Music can awaken us. But for Cathy, it could also undo her.

13

The "Kiss of God"

Some moments arrive so quietly, yet leave a mark so deep, it feels like something sacred has brushed against you. For Mukundan, those moments came not in dreams or visions — but in the soft ringing of temple bells.

He was forty-two, a taxi driver from Sri Lanka who had built a quiet life in Canada. The kind of man who smiled easily, prayed every night, and believed that faith could keep the darkness at bay.

It was his wife, Suchitra, who first noticed the change.

"Doctor," she said, her voice trembling, "whenever we go to the temple, he starts to… change. He closes his eyes, tears fall, his body shakes. He says it's a blessing. But I'm scared."

When Mukundan came to see me, he sat calmly — palms resting on his knees, his eyes bright with something that felt halfway between peace and awe.

"Doctor," he said softly, "when the bells ring and the hymns begin, I feel it here." He touched his chest. "A warmth. Like sunlight spreading through me. It feels as if the Goddess is kissing me… like my mother's love wrapping around me. For a few seconds, everything disappears — fear, noise, pain — and only joy remains."

To the priest, it was divine, to his wife, it was frightening. To science, it was something else.

When Mukundan's brain activity was recorded on an EEG, the mystery deepened — and clarified. The blissful moments he described matched sudden, sharp bursts of electrical activity in his **right insular cortex** — the region that weaves together emotion, awareness, and spiritual feeling.

It wasn't madness. And it wasn't a miracle in the way most imagine. It was a rare phenomenon known as **ecstatic epilepsy** — a kind of seizure that doesn't bring pain or confusion, but a flood of euphoria so pure it feels like touching the divine.

I told him gently, "Mukundan, this isn't a curse. And it isn't just a blessing, either. What you feel is real — but it begins inside your own mind. A spark, a surge, a brief song of neurons. It doesn't make your faith smaller. If anything, it shows how wondrous the human brain truly is."

Mukundan smiled then — slow, knowing. The truth hadn't broken his faith. It had given it shape.

14

Menu Cards That Make You Faint

He was the kind of man who looked like he had his life together — tall, well-groomed, the kind of quiet presence that made you think of calm seas. But when Peter spoke, you could feel the storm beneath.

His wife, Cecilia, sat beside him — graceful, patient, eyes full of love and exhaustion. When she spoke, her voice trembled in that way people sound when they've been strong for too long.

I asked softly, "Peter, what brings you here?"

He smiled faintly — a sad, self-aware smile. "Doctor," he said, "if you think this is small, I promise you it's not. I can't make decisions."

He paused, searching for words. "Even choosing a shirt… I can spend an hour. Choosing a meal, a movie, a word to say — I go in circles. My mind won't stop weighing, comparing, doubting. I'm trapped inside it."

Cecilia's eyes lowered. Her fingers twisted the edge of her scarf. "I love him," she said quietly. "But I'm tired. I never know when a simple question — dinner, or what to wear — will turn into hours of silence."

Peter nodded. "The other night," he whispered, "she asked what I wanted for dinner. Pasta, pizza, salad — and I froze. The clock kept ticking. She went to bed hungry. I just sat there, still deciding." He took a breath. "Once, I fainted in a restaurant. I'd stared at the menu for too long. My brain just… shut down."

It wasn't laziness. It wasn't pride. It was a mind at war with itself — a rare condition called **aboulomania**. A paralysis of decision, where every choice splits into endless possibilities, and every possibility feels like a trap. Perfection becomes a cage.

"Peter," I said gently, "your brain isn't broken. It's just afraid — afraid of being wrong. We'll start small. One choice at a time."

And so we did. Therapy began — slow, careful, patient. Cognitive-behavioral exercises, breathing, small daily decisions. Cecilia became his anchor, steady and unyielding in the storm.

Weeks passed. One day, at his final session, I placed two pens on the table — one black, one red.

"Peter," I said, "pick one."

He stared at them, silent. A single second stretched into many. Then he reached out and picked the black pen.

He smiled — small, trembling, proud. "Even if it's the wrong one," he said, "I choose this."

I nodded. "Then it's the right attitude."

Cecilia's eyes filled with tears — not sadness, but relief.

15

Soap Eaters

She walked in slowly, as if every step carried a secret. Mira — twenty-two, a medical student — bright mind, quiet eyes. Her hands clung to the strap of her bag like it was something to hold her steady.

Behind her came her mother — a university professor, calm in posture but breaking inside. "Doctor," she said, her voice tight with control, "she has a problem. She only came because I made her."

I motioned for them to sit. The clock ticked. Then silence. Until the mother spoke again. "She eats things… things that aren't food. Chalk. Paper. Bits of soil."

Mira flinched, then whispered, "It's true." Her words trembled in the air.
"I don't know when it started. Maybe when I was six. I remember the smell of chalk in the classroom. It was clean, soft. I touched it to my tongue once — just once. Then I hid pieces in my pocket. Took them home. Later, it was paper, soil, little bits of wood. I couldn't stop."

She looked up, eyes shining with shame. "When I eat them… I feel calm. Like something inside me finally quiets down. But I know it's wrong. I even wanted to eat soap once. I tried. I got so sick, I couldn't breathe. My mother had to take me to the hospital."

Her mother's voice cracked for the first time. "She was in pain for hours. I thought I'd lose her."

I took a breath. "Mira, this isn't your fault. What you have is called *Pica.* It makes people crave things that aren't food — chalk, soil, paper. It's not a bad habit. It's a signal. Your body might be missing nutrients, like iron or zinc."

Her eyes widened. "So… I'm not losing my mind?"

"No," I said softly. "Your body is asking for help, not punishment. Even today, in many countries, pregnant women crave chalk or clay — it's a response to nutrient changes. You're not alone in this."

Over the next few sessions, Mira started keeping a journal. Every craving, every urge, every time she gave in or didn't. Blood tests confirmed what I suspected — low iron, low zinc. We began supplements, and small steps to retrain her body and mind.

"When you feel the craving," I told her, "Try something else. Something safe. Chocolate. Fruit. Chewing gum. It's not about stopping yourself — it's about giving your body what it truly needs."

Weeks passed. Then one day, she came back — a faint smile flickering across her face.

"Doctor," she said quietly, "I saw the chalk today. I didn't want it. Not even a little."

Her mother exhaled, her voice softer than I'd ever heard it. "She's lighter now. She laughs again."

I smiled. "That's what recovery sounds like, Mira. Remember — Pica isn't a weakness. It's a whisper from the body about some deficiencies. And you've learned how to listen."

16

Sir- the Holy Spirit

She sat before me, wrapped in a black scarf that swallowed half her face. Amina. Thirty-two. From Sudan. Two years in Canada, and already carrying a silence that felt centuries old.

Her hands were clasped so tightly that her knuckles had turned white — as if she were trying to hold herself together.

When she finally spoke, her voice was a thread of air. "Doctor," she said, "there's something inside me."

I leaned forward, lowering my voice. "You can speak freely here. You're safe."

For a long moment, she said nothing. Then, slowly, she loosened the scarf. Her eyes met mine — dark, alive, and full of terror.

"It comes without warning," she whispered. "Like heat rising from the ground. My chest tightens, my hands shake. I can feel it… moving through me."

Her husband, who sat in the corner, spoke in a low voice. "When it happens, she doesn't recognize me. She speaks to someone who isn't there. She says she smells it — the spirit."

Amina nodded. "It's true. I feel it breathing inside me. It calls my name." She pressed a trembling hand against her chest. "Here. It lives here."

In her village, this was not an illness — it was a visitation. When the spirit came, the women would gather. Drums would echo through the night, feet stamping, voices rising — a ritual called Zār. It was not a curse but a communion.

"When the drums played," she said softly, her eyes far away, "I was strong. Respected. Not afraid. But here…" Her voice faltered.

"Here, they say I'm unwell. They call it madness."

I waited, then spoke gently. "Amina, what you feel is real. But it isn't a curse, and you are not broken. The mind can carry pain in strange ways. In your village, it was called a spirit. Here, it has another name — trauma, memory, grief. But it's still your pain asking to be heard."

Her eyes filled. "So it's not me?"

"No," I said quietly. "It's something you've carried for too long. It doesn't want to destroy you — it wants to be seen."

She wept then, softly, like someone finally allowed to breathe. Over the next few months, she came back again and again. We spoke about fear, about memory, about what cannot be buried. She learned to face the presence, not run from it. To let it exist without letting it rule.

And one afternoon, she walked in — no scarf this time. Her hands were calm. Her eyes, steady.

"Doctor," she said, "the spirit… it doesn't visit anymore."

I smiled. "Maybe it finally found peace." And sometimes, what we call a spirit is only our pain, waiting to be named.

17

Those Who Love the Aggressor

Sania was just twenty, a brilliant young mind, an engineering student hailing from Afghanistan. Recently, she had been pulled from a kidnapping, a terror no one should have to know. When she was finally safe, the world waited for a scream, a sob, for the storm of trauma. What came instead was a stillness, a shock of calm.

"They mustn't hurt him," she kept insisting. "Leave him be. He is a decent man."

Her family, the officers, even the judge—all were left baffled. She simply would not testify against the man who had taken her. It was this silence that brought her to my quiet little office.

The first time she sat across from me, she seemed so small. Her hands were locked together, her gaze fixed to the floorboards. The air was thick with a strange tension, the way fragility and unseen strength can hang together like a heavy fog.

I leaned closer. My voice was very gentle. "Sania… what's stirring inside you right now?"

Her eyes flickered up, a tremor running through her. "Everyone believes I should despise him," she breathed. "They want him put away. But... I don't feel he's bad. He never harmed me. Somehow… he made me feel secure. More secure than I ever felt at home."

Tears made slow, wet tracks down her face. I didn't rush her. I let her find the courage to begin the story. Her words came out slowly, like delicate threads of memory being unspooled.

"I was at the university, having coffee," she began. "He approached and said he needed to show me something crucial. He claimed… my mother was waiting in his car. I thought something urgent had happened, so I trusted him and followed. Then, suddenly, he shoved me inside. My hands were tied, my eyes covered. I thought I would surely suffocate... that I was going to die."

She took a shuddering breath. "But… after a while, he soothed me. He gave me a meal and a drink. He spoke softly. He never raised his voice. He never hit me. Bit by bit… the fear shifted. I felt… that he was the only one who could save me, perhaps because there was truly no one else nearby."

Her father, sitting stiffly beside her, shook his head in absolute disbelief. "Doctor… what kind of insanity is this? He is a criminal! And she… she views him as a guardian?"

I raised a hand, keeping my tone steady. "Allow me to explain," I told him.

I turned back to Sania. "Tell me more about him."

"He truly listened to my words," she said, her voice shaking slightly. "He shared stories. He made jokes. He told me he came from a life of hardship, of hunger and poverty. I know he needed money, and this… was the only route he understood. Please… don't ruin what little chance he has."

I nodded slowly, letting the gravity of her confession settle. "Sania, what you feel is profoundly real. The emotion is absolutely genuine. It's born from your experience. But it doesn't undo the crime. Legally, he kidnapped you. He must face the consequences. What you are experiencing now… it is your mind's way of ensuring survival. It has a name: Stockholm Syndrome."

Her eyes widened, as if a profound and terrible secret had just been revealed.

"Stockholm Syndrome occurs when a person is held captive, utterly helpless. The mind forms a connection with the person who holds power—a strange blend of terror, reliance, and yes… even kindness. It's a defense mechanism, a tool to avoid further injury. A path to survival. With time, as the real world returns, these feelings will quietly dissolve."

Her tears fell. "So… I am not losing my mind?"

"Never," I promised. "This is simply your mind keeping you alive. You are secure now. The greatest gift is that no true trauma seems to be clinging to you. That is all that matters. Empathy, patience, and time will handle the rest."

The weeks turned into months. Sania came back again and again, her quiet strength growing. The shadow that had followed her slowly began to withdraw. And as she left my office for the final time, I understood something extraordinary: the mind's incredible will to survive, even if it has to weave a strange kind of bond out of fear and affection, just to endure.

18

Those Who Beat Themselves

I remember the first time I met Leo. He was twelve — small for his age, fragile as a paper bird. His wheelchair looked too large for him, as though it belonged to someone else. Soft pads were wrapped around his wrists, not to trap him, but to keep him safe from his own strength.

His eyes were calm pools, wide and dark — the kind that hold both light and sorrow at once. Behind him stood his mother, Maria. Her hands rested gently on his shoulders, steady but trembling with exhaustion.

"Go on, sweetheart," she whispered. "You can talk to the doctor."

I knelt so we were eye to eye. "What did you eat this morning, Leo?"

He smiled — a shy, careful smile. "Toast. And eggs." His voice was soft, polite, so normal that for a moment, I almost forgot why he was there.

Then Maria's hands slipped away.

It happened in a blink. Leo's right hand shot up and struck his cheek. A sharp crack echoed through the room — small, but it felt enormous.

Maria gasped, gathering him close. "It's alright, baby," she whispered, her voice breaking. "It's not your fault."

Leo's face twisted, not in pain — but in confusion. "Doctor," he said, his lip trembling, "my hands… they don't listen to me."

Before I could answer, his fingers moved again — turning against him, desperate and wild. Maria caught them, pressing them to her chest as tears slipped silently down her face.

I spoke softly. "Does this happen often?"

She nodded. "Every day. He bites himself. Hits himself. He doesn't want to, but he can't stop. They said it's called *Lesch-Nyhan syndrome.* They said it's rare. But no one told me how it feels… watching your child fight his own body."

Leo looked up at me, eyes full of fear and hope tangled together. "Can you make me stop? Can you make my hands listen?"

There are questions no doctor ever gets used to hearing.

I took his hand, small and trembling, and said quietly, "Leo, this isn't your fault. Your brain sends signals it shouldn't — like a wire crossed in a machine. It makes your body move before you can think. But we can help. We can make the war inside you a little quieter."

He blinked hard. "Sometimes… I hit my mom too," he whispered. "I hate it."

Maria leaned closer, her tears steady but calm. "I know, my love. And I know it's not you."

We began with small things — soft rubber balls for him to squeeze, medicines to calm the storms, moments of stillness that slowly grew longer. Five minutes of peace became ten. Then fifteen.

And then one afternoon, Leo laughed — freely, without fear — as if his hands had finally forgiven him.

The bruises faded. The guilt eased.

Lesch-Nyhan syndrome is indeed a rare, inherited disorder caused by a deficiency of the enzyme *HPRT (hypoxanthine-guanine phosphoribosyltransferase).*

It causes neurological and behavioral symptoms, including self-injury, due to dysfunction in brain regions controlling movement and impulse

It tricks the brain into turning against the body. But even in that betrayal, love found a way to stay. Maria never gave up. And Leo, piece by piece, learned how to live with what his body could not control.

When I think of them now, I see a small candle burning in a room full of shadows — trembling, but never giving in.

19

The Taste of Heaven

Tommy sat by the window as dawn unfolded quietly. The first rays of sunlight slipped through the glass, brushing against the old wooden table. A cup of tea steamed beside the newspaper—an ordinary morning, peaceful and predictable.

And yet, that morning, something changed. He was reading, half-aware of the words, when a strange warmth bloomed inside his chest. His breath slowed. His fingers loosened their grip on the paper. The room seemed to soften—edges fading, colors melting into a golden haze.

For a brief, shimmering moment, he wasn't sitting in his chair anymore. He was floating. Weightless. The world around him disappeared, replaced by an overwhelming sense of joy—pure, wordless and infinite.

Later, when he came to see me, his hands were trembling. "Doctor," he whispered, "I felt like I was melting into the universe. The trees, the stars, the air… everything was part of me. I've prayed, I've meditated, but this—this was different. For a second, I tasted heaven."

For Tommy, it was divine—a secret touch from the beyond. For science, it was something else entirely.

Deep within the brain lies the limbic system—the keeper of emotions, memory, and meaning. Sometimes, when its circuits flare in unexpected harmony, consciousness can shift. The boundaries between self and world blur. For some, it feels like God's embrace; for others, like dissolving into nature—a light that whispers love, a peace that surpasses reason.

A gentle nun once told me her own story in hushed tones.

"When it happens," she said, "I hear the trees speaking. Once, a golden light came close… and it said, 'You are loved. You are needed.' Doctor, I've never been that happy. I'd give anything to feel it again."

I explained softly, "It might be a kind of temporal lobe storm—an electrical surge in the brain."

She only smiled. Not in disbelief, but in quiet knowing. "Call it what you wish," she said. "To me, it's a gift. Who wouldn't want to touch heaven, even for a moment?"

History remembers others who felt the same—poets, nuns, painters, even prophets—each claiming to have brushed against eternity.

Fyodor Dostoevsky once wrote,

"I sometimes feel a sense of oneness with my body and the universe. I would give ten years—perhaps my whole life—for this bliss that lasts only a few seconds."

Whether it begins in the folds of the brain or in the hand of the divine, light still feels like light. And sometimes, just a few seconds of that light are enough to change everything.

"Perhaps heaven is not a place we go to—but a moment that finds us when the soul forgets to be afraid."

20

The Song That Opened Heaven

Gordon was an ordinary man. He worked as a security guard, came home to his wife and children, and sang in the church choir every Sunday. He was steady, kind, and simple. But there was one song—one hymn—that changed everything.

No one could explain what it did to him. Each Sunday, when the organist played the first three notes, something inside Gordon broke open. His wife noticed it first.

"Doctor," she whispered once, her voice trembling, "he goes still for half a minute. Then he leans against the pew—pale, shaking, his eyes… they're empty. Like he's not in this world at all."

Gordon remembered the feeling. "A wave would rise inside me," he said. "From my stomach to my throat. Like stepping out of a fast elevator, or falling—but upward. The church, the candles, the people—they all disappeared. Even the sound vanished. It was like slipping into another place."

The congregation whispered that he had been *touched by the Spirit.* But the doctors thought otherwise.

At the hospital, we played the same hymn again. Within seconds, his EEG came alive. Spikes of electricity flared in his right temporal lobe—then a storm. Gordon's eyes rolled back. He collapsed. The machine caught every spark, every surge—a vision of heaven flickering inside his brain.

He had a rare brain condition called *focal cortical dysplasia*, a tiny flaw in the wiring of his temporal lobe. The hymn had once been his mother's favourite. Her voice, her presence, her love—all lived in that melody. Each time he heard it, her memory struck something deep within him, triggering the seizure.

"It wasn't just a song," Gordon said later, his voice low. "It was *her*. Every note felt like she was calling me back. I couldn't stop it."

After surgery, the storms went silent. A month later, Gordon returned to church. The organ began to play the same hymn. This time—no trembling, no collapse, no light behind his eyes. Just tears. Quiet, grateful tears.

He sang louder than anyone that morning—his voice steady, human, free.

Somewhere between science and mystery lies a place where the soul and the brain meet. Understanding it doesn't take away its wonder—it helps us see it more clearly.

21

The Second Life of Paul

It began like a faint ripple at the edge of his thoughts.

Paul, a forty-year-old history professor, wasn't remembering the past. He was *living* it—stepping into a world that felt achingly familiar, yet entirely foreign.

When it happened, his eyes lost focus. His breath grew still. The room around him faded, as though someone had turned the world's volume down to a whisper.

For a few minutes, Paul was gone. He walked through a life that wasn't his—streets that glistened after rain, the salt of the ocean on his lips, a woman's laughter carried by the wind. Every detail was sharp, alive, and heartbreakingly real. Then, just as suddenly, it was gone.

"Doctor," he said once, clutching a weathered notebook, "I'm not imagining this. I'm *in Rio*. I feel the rain on my face. I see a yellow Fiat. I married someone there. I died there. I *felt* it happen."

He filled notebook after notebook, pages dense with names, maps, and memories that no one else could confirm. His sister's voice trembled as she told me, "We checked. None of it's real. But for him—it is."

This wasn't madness or a dream. It was a seizure—an electrical storm in the temporal lobe, the brain's memory center. During those moments, his neurons sparked in patterns so vivid they built entire lives from nothing.

"Paul," I told him softly, "your brain isn't remembering another life. It's *creating* one."

He looked at me as if I'd told him the world he'd built was dust. But there was no cruelty in the truth. Just wonder—and the eerie power of a mind that could bend time and memory at will.

Epileptic déjà vu is a real phenomenon—a form of déjà vu that happens during a temporal lobe seizure.

For most people, déjà vu is a fleeting quirk of memory, harmless and forgettable. But in epilepsy, it can be a signal—a brief surge of abnormal electrical activity in the brain. It often comes with a rush of emotion, a sense of being pulled somewhere both known and impossible.

People may feel:

- A sudden wave of fear or familiarity
- A strange rising in the stomach
- Distorted time, space, or sound
- Scents or tastes that appear out of nowhere

The episode lasts only seconds or a minute, but it can feel like eternity. When it passes, exhaustion or confusion often follows.

Doctors confirm it with EEG and MRI scans, and it's treated like other types of epilepsy—usually with anti-seizure medication, and sometimes surgery if needed.

The temporal lobe, where memory and emotion intertwine, is both fragile and powerful. When its circuits misfire, it can project an entire life into existence—real enough to break your heart, yet gone before you can take a breath.

For a moment after he spoke, the room was still. Between us hung the echo of rain on streets he had never walked, the scent of an ocean he had never seen.

And I thought—maybe what he saw wasn't madness at all, but the mind showing us how thin the walls of reality truly are.

22

When Songs Become Villains

She sat across from me, her hands trembling slightly, the sunlight trembling with them. Helen had once been composed—measured, bright, grounded in the ordinary rhythm of life. But that morning, she looked like someone who had stepped out of a dream and wasn't sure if she'd truly woken up.

"Doctor," she whispered, "something strange happens when I hear a certain song… my lips start to move, my fingers shake. I don't control it. It's as if… the music is inside me, moving me."

I watched her carefully. There was fear, yes—but not the kind born from pain or illness. It was the fear of losing trust in one's own self. The fear that the familiar world had turned into something unrecognizable.

We searched for reasons. Seizure medications failed her. Silence offered no mercy. Yet the pattern was unmistakable—every time that melody returned, her body obeyed it like a forgotten ritual.

Then came the revelation. Her blood held a secret—a flood of antibodies called **anti-AAU65**, attacking her own brain. The body, confused in its sacred duty, had mistaken self for enemy. Her movements were not born of madness, but of mistaken defence—an invisible rebellion within.

"Helen," I said softly, "the brain is like an orchestra, every note in harmony. But when these antibodies appear, they silence the conductor. The music that should comfort you now commands you. Your body becomes the instrument, and the melody… plays you."

Her eyes widened, glistening with both wonder and sorrow. "So the song is alive inside me?"

"In a way," I said. "It isn't the song that's alive—it's you. But for a while, the two became one."

She began treatment—steroids, rest, the slow unwinding of chaos. And in time, the storm within her quieted. One day, she walked into a small café, sunlight spilling across the tables. She placed her headphones on and pressed play. The same song that once ruled her body now floated through her gently—no tremors, no fear. Just sound, and peace.

She smiled. The villain had turned back into music. Sometimes, the body rebels so fiercely that it steals the voice of the soul. And sometimes, healing is not about silencing the noise—but learning how to listen again.

23

When Images Speak to the Brain

Sometimes, an image doesn't just reach the eyes — it goes straight to the brain, whispering louder than any sound, faster than any thought.

I've seen it happen. A photograph, a flash of light, a simple pattern — and suddenly, the mind begins to tremble. These aren't ghosts or illusions. They are real storms — silent, electrical, and terrifyingly precise.

Case 1: Arjun and the Portrait

Arjun was fifteen. Bright, polite, curious. He loved old photos — school pictures, family albums, even old newspapers.

One afternoon, his father rushed into my clinic, voice shaking. "Doctor," he said, "when Arjun looks at certain photographs, he… changes. His eyes go wide, his hands shake, and then he collapses. It's always the same — especially with black-and-white portraits."

Arjun sat beside him, pale but calm. "The first time," he said, "I was looking at my old teacher's picture. She had died a few months before. I felt dizzy — then everything went dark."

His mother's voice was barely a whisper. "We thought it was a coincidence. But it happened again — scrolling through Facebook. Now we can't even open a photo album without fear."

In the hospital, we ran an EEG — a test that records brain activity. As Arjun looked at a series of simple portraits, the screen suddenly lit up with sharp waves. His brain had erupted in the occipital lobe — the region that turns light into vision.

His MRI was clear. No injury. No tumor. Just a brain tuned too finely — like an instrument that reacts to every vibration.

I explained quietly, "This is called **photogenic epilepsy**. For some people, certain images — strong patterns, colors, contrasts — can overstimulate the brain's visual center. That overload becomes a seizure."

His mother frowned. "Like the kind caused by TV lights?" "Yes," I said. "But in his case, even a still photograph can do it."

For most of us, the world is a gallery of memories. For Arjun, it had become a minefield. One image could pull him into darkness.

Case 2: Ali and the Flash of Light

Ali was sixteen, from Iran — shy, thoughtful, a boy who loved music. His mother told me, "The first time it happened, we were at a concert. A bright flash hit his eyes. He froze… then fell. We thought it was shock. But it happened again — watching videos online."

His brain wasn't afraid of the world. It was reacting to it. Light itself was his trigger — a camera flash, sunlight flickering through trees, reflections off a lake. Any burst could switch off his world for seconds.

Ali had **photosensitive epilepsy** — a condition where flashing or flickering light causes the brain's visual circuits to misfire. For most people, those lights are harmless. For him, they were thunderclaps in the dark.

Case 3: The Pokémon Incident

And then, there was the night Japan fell silent. In 1997, during an episode of a popular cartoon, a scene flashed red and blue lights in rapid bursts. Within minutes, hundreds of children across the country collapsed. Some vomited, others fainted, many were rushed to hospitals.

It wasn't the story that hurt them — it was the light. Those flashes overloaded their **visual cortex**, setting off seizures in more than 680 children. One moment of animation had reached straight into their brains and flipped a hidden switch.

The Invisible Language of Light

Not every brain sees the same world. For some, light and pattern are more than beauty — they're codes, keys that can unlock storms hidden deep inside.

Roughly one in every four thousand people has this kind of sensitivity. The **occipital lobe**, the part that lets us see, can be like dry leaves — one spark, and it catches fire.

But knowing this doesn't take away its mystery. It only reminds us how delicate perception really is — how easily the mind can turn light into thunder.

For those who live with it, every reflection, every flicker, every glowing screen is both a window and a warning.

24

The King Liar

"The first time Jennifer walked into my consulting room, I remember thinking she looked like someone who had just stepped out of a movie. Her perfume drifted softly in the air, her hair perfectly arranged, and in her hands, she held a small, elegant box as if it contained something sacred. Every detail about her — from the silk scarf around her neck to the way she crossed her legs — spoke of quiet sophistication.

She smiled and said with calm authority, "Doctor, I suppose you've heard of me. I'm a Canadian diplomat. I've lived in Moscow, Beijing, and a few other places you've probably only seen on television."

Her tone was so natural, so practiced, that for a moment even I found myself leaning in.

"That must have been quite an adventure," I said. "What was Moscow like?"

Her eyes brightened. "Moscow was dangerous," she whispered, almost proudly. "You have to be clever to survive there. The CIA once tried to recruit me. They wanted secrets."

I listened, quietly.

"And Beijing?" I asked.

She smiled wistfully. "Ah, Beijing was… kind. The Chinese respected me. Hu Jintao himself invited me to dinner — many times."

Hu Jintao. The former Chinese President. She said it so effortlessly, as if recalling a familiar dinner companion.

I didn't challenge her. People like Jennifer live inside stories that shimmer with conviction. To question them too early is to shatter a fragile world they've built with trembling hands.

Later that day, when I opened her file, I found something that struck me harder than any diagnosis. There were no stamps in her passport. No records of diplomatic service. No foreign travel.

Jennifer had never left Canada. Every tale she told — Moscow, Beijing, the CIA — was spun from pure imagination.

But she wasn't a fraud. She wasn't trying to deceive or steal or manipulate. She lied because her stories gave her something life had not: importance, meaning, and escape. For her, those lies were not weapons — they were lifeboats.

As our sessions went on, I began to see the quiet ache behind her confident smile. Jennifer's life had once been ordinary, painfully so. She had dreamed of greatness, but the world had handed her smallness instead. So, piece by piece, she built a new life — one that existed only in words but felt truer than the world around her.

She wasn't pretending anymore. She had started believing fragments of her own stories.

Her brain scans were clear. No tumor. No lesions. No sign of psychosis. This wasn't a disorder of the brain — it was a wound of the heart.

One day, I asked her softly, "Jennifer, when you tell these stories… do they make the world feel a little better?"

She looked down, her voice barely a breath. "They make me feel like I exist."

PSEUDOLOGIA FANTASTICA

In psychiatry, this condition is known as **pseudologia fantastica** — pathological lying. It isn't recognized as a separate disease but as a behavior pattern often seen in personality disorders like narcissistic, borderline, histrionic, or factitious disorders.

Key traits clinicians look for include:

- **Persistent, elaborate fabrications:** stories may span entire careers, families, or lifetimes.
- **Emotional motive:** lies often protect fragile self-worth or help the person feel admired or special.
- **Partial insight:** when confronted, some acknowledge the falsehood; others cling to it.
- **Early onset:** the pattern usually begins in adolescence and continues for years.

Pathological lying isn't always about deceiving others — sometimes, it's about surviving oneself. When reality feels too small, some people build kingdoms in their minds… and move in.

Behind the perfect smile and the diplomat's grace, Jennifer wasn't a manipulator. She was simply a woman longing to be seen.

25

The World Without Faces

The rain that morning was soft — the kind that doesn't fall, but whispers.

Benton stood by the window, buttoning his coat, the familiar weight of his violin case at his side. As he reached for his hat, his fingers brushed against something warm. Soft. Alive.

"Benton?" came a gentle voice. "What are you doing?"

He froze. His hand rested on his wife's head. He hadn't meant to touch her. He had mistaken her face… for his hat.

Benton was no ordinary man. He was a musician whose fingers could summon silence from a crowd — a genius who could make violins weep and cellos breathe. But now, faces — the most human of all images — had vanished from his world.

When doctors placed family photos before him, his responses were heartbreaking in their strangeness.

"This one," he said, pointing at a photograph of his son, "looks like… a mirror."

"And this?" they asked.

"A coat. Or maybe a window frame. Something familiar — but not someone."

In Benton's eyes, faces had shattered into pieces — an eyebrow floating like a bird, a mouth like a curved line drawn by mistake. He could see, yet he could not *know*. He began to recognize people by their rhythms — the sound of a voice, the tilt of a head, the way someone's footsteps carried their mood.

His brain scans revealed the quiet culprit: damage to the right occipital–temporal region, the part that turns fragments into faces.

The rest of his mind was untouched — his memory, his music, his imagination — all intact. But the world he saw was now a stage full of masks without meaning.

"I see faces," Benton once told Oliver Sacks. "But I have no names. No souls behind them. Only shapes that pretend to be human."

The Masked Classroom

When Alicia returned to her classroom after the accident, the children stood to greet her, their voices warm and bright. But to her, it was like walking into a masquerade — every child hidden behind an unfamiliar mask.

She smiled at a girl in the front row. "Good morning, Mina," she said softly.

The girl frowned. Because she wasn't Mina at all. Every face in that room was a stranger's. Even her husband's face in photographs had become a blank surface — familiar and foreign at once. But when he spoke, his voice reached her like light through fog. The sound, the smell of his cologne, the way his fingers brushed hers — these became her map back to love.

Doctors showed her scans of her brain. The right fusiform gyrus — the area that recognizes faces — had gone dark. Her vision was perfect. Her mind, sharp as ever. But the bridge between seeing and knowing had been quietly broken.

"I am learning to live in a world without faces," she said softly. "A world where everyone is a stranger… until they speak."

Prosopagnosia

There is a name for this haunting condition: Prosopagnosia — face blindness. It is not the eyes that fail, nor the memory that fades. It is the mind's silent artist — the *fusiform gyrus* — that forgets how to draw the most familiar portrait of all: the human face.

A stroke. A head injury. Or sometimes, a pattern written into the brain from birth — any of these can cause faces to break apart into meaningless fragments. The eyes, the mouth, the skin — they're all there, but they never come together to form *someone.*

Those who live with this condition walk through the world like travelers at a masked carnival. They identify others by their voices, their laughter, their scent, or the rhythm of their steps. They live surrounded by people they love deeply — yet can no longer recognize by sight.

But here lies the strange beauty of their world. Stripped of faces, they begin to see what lies beneath them — tone, kindness, presence, the things most of us overlook.

Perhaps, in losing the image of faces, they learn to see the

26

Who Am I?

The street was hushed that evening, the kind of silence that hides secrets behind every breath. Two policemen walked down the dim lanes of Gwalior, weary after a long day. Near a cracked wall, a beggar lay curled up on the cold pavement—his beard tangled, his clothes hanging loose, his face just another forgotten one.

They might have walked past him forever—if he hadn't whispered their names.

"Ravi… Mohan."

The sound was faint, almost fragile, but it stopped them cold. The two officers turned, uneasy, as if the past had just spoken from the shadows.

"Who are you?" Mohan asked. The man lifted his head slowly. "Manish Mishra."

The name fell heavy between them. It wasn't a stranger's name—it was a memory. A friend. A fellow officer who had vanished a decade ago without a trace.

Manish Mishra, once a sharpshooter of the Madhya Pradesh Police, had disappeared one morning and was never found. Now he sat before them, not as a hero in uniform, but as a nameless beggar who couldn't remember who he was.

For ten long years, Manish had wandered the streets, speaking like any man, walking like any man—but knowing nothing of himself. His mind had erased his story to protect what was left of it.

The Forgotten Engineer

Across the city, beneath the flickering yellow lights of a bus stand, social workers found another lost soul. He was old, almost ninety.

His voice was calm, his English sharp and precise—too precise for a man in rags.

"My name..." he began, and then stopped. "I don't know."

He was later identified as **Surendra Vasishth**, once a mechanical engineer from the Indian Institute of Technology, Kanpur. Later, a lawyer. A man of brilliance and purpose.

But somewhere along life's winding path, something inside him had quietly broken. His mind had folded in on itself, erasing his identity to protect what his heart could no longer carry. He had lived as a wanderer, stripped of everything but breath.

Becoming Someone Else

And far away, in another century, another man forgot himself too. His name was **Ansel Bourne**, a preacher and carpenter from Rhode Island.

On a winter morning in 1887, he left home without saying a word. Days turned into weeks. When he opened his eyes again, he was in Pennsylvania—living under a new name, **J. Brown**.

He rented a small shop, sold candies, spoke to neighbours, and built a new life without ever knowing it wasn't truly his. To everyone else, he seemed normal. To himself, he was complete.

Six weeks later, he saw a poster with his real name on it—**Ansel Bourne Missing**—and something inside him cracked open. The memories came flooding back, wild and unstoppable. He sat down on a bench, trembling. "Who was I all this time?" he whispered. "And who am I now?"

Who am I?

Manish. Surendra. Ansel. Three lives. Three disappearances. One strange truth.

What they suffered is called **dissociative fugue**—a rare, mysterious condition where the mind, unable to bear pain or trauma, simply walks away from itself.

The body remains. The skills remain. But the self—the name, the past, the life story—vanishes, leaving behind a person without a history.

Sometimes, memory returns suddenly—through a smell, a familiar face, or a forgotten song. Sometimes, it creeps back in fragments. And sometimes… it never returns at all.

This forgetting is not cruelty. It is protection. When pain becomes unbearable, the mind chooses to survive by erasing the self.

What it feels like:

- The name disappears. The address, the family, the story—all gone.
- Yet the feet keep moving—buying bus tickets, finding food, renting rooms.
- To strangers, you seem normal. To yourself, you are no one.
- Only the present moment feels real; the past is a blank wall.

Why it happens: Fugue is the mind's emergency escape hatch, triggered by deep trauma, shame, or unbearable stress. It can follow:

- Childhood abuse or battlefield horror
- Sudden loss, divorce, or humiliation
- Severe depression or PTSD

The Way Back

Recovery begins with safety—with gentle reminders of the life once lived: familiar scents, old photographs, a song once loved.

There is no medicine to cure fugue—only time, compassion, and therapy once the memories return. And sometimes, in the quiet of one night's sleep, it happens all at once—the forgotten story rushes back like a river breaking through stone.

"I left myself," one patient said, "to survive myself."

Somewhere, deep within the silent corners of every mind, the forgotten self waits—patient, watchful, like a locked room whose key lies hidden in plain sight.

"Memory is the diary we all carry about with us." — Oscar Wilde

27

Fight in Their Sleep

The clock on the wall had just crossed eight. I was about to close my consultation room when a soft knock came at the door. The nurse peeked in, her voice barely above a whisper. "Doctor… there's one more case."

A small girl walked in with her parents. Her name was **Haya**—twelve years old, fragile, with dark eyes that looked far older than her years. She clung to her mother's shawl, as if the world outside frightened her. Her parents, an Egyptian couple, looked worn out—their faces pale, their eyes red from nights without rest.

The mother began to speak, her voice trembling. "Doctor, every night it happens. She fights something in her sleep. Sometimes she jumps out of bed, screaming. We've locked every door, every window. We're terrified."

The father nodded slowly. "At first, we thought it was stress from school. Then nightmares. Then sleepwalking. We tried everything. But it happens every night. When she wakes, she remembers nothing—only feels so tired she can hardly keep her eyes open in class."

The mother's hands shook as she continued. "Fifteen minutes after falling asleep, her eyes open wide. Her arms jerk, her legs thrash. She screams… but it doesn't sound like her. It sounds like someone else."

The episodes were brief—less than a minute—but came again and again, every night. By morning, the child was exhausted, her small body bruised by sleep itself.

A Trail of Misunderstandings

Their family doctor had brushed it off. "Just stress," he'd said. A few pills, a few comforting words—but nothing changed.

Later, a psychologist saw what others didn't—a shadow deeper than dreams—and sent her to us, to watch the night more closely.

When the Night Was Watched

We admitted Haya for a **sleep study**. A small room, silent except for the hum of machines. Electrodes touched her scalp like silver threads, tracing her brain's secret language.

For a while, everything was peaceful. Then it began.

A twitch, a sudden jerk. Her arms flung out, her legs kicked, her mouth opened into a cry that seemed to rise from somewhere far beyond the walls.

On the EEG screen, small bursts of electricity flickered in her **frontal lobe**—the part of the brain that controls movement. Her body and her brain were speaking the same language now. This wasn't fear, wasn't a dream. This was her brain misfiring in the dark.

The Name of the Enemy

The next morning, I sat with her parents. Their faces were pale, but they listened with quiet strength.

"This," I said softly, "is a rare condition called **Sleep-Related Hypermotor Epilepsy**."

They looked at me, confused.

"When Haya falls asleep," I explained, "a small part of her brain wakes up and sends chaotic signals to her body. The movements—the cries—they're **seizures**, not nightmares. She isn't aware of them. It's not in her mind—it's in her brain. And yes, it can be treated."

The mother's eyes filled with tears. "So… she isn't dreaming?"

"No," I said. "Her dreams are innocent. It's her brain that's been fighting. But we can help her rest again."

A long silence followed—one heavy with relief. After years of fear, the enemy had finally been given a name.

The Road Back

Medication came first—gentle, steady, precise. Counseling, understanding, and support followed close behind. In rare cases, a small surgery can quiet the electrical storm forever.

But that night, the greatest medicine wasn't in a tablet. It was **understanding**—the moment when fear turns into knowledge, and darkness begins to lift.

In time, Haya would sleep again—peacefully, safely, like every child should.

"Some battles are not fought in daylight, but in dreams."

28

Orgasams knock you down

They entered the room like two shadows stitched together by silence — a husband and wife who seemed to be carrying something fragile between them, something neither had dared to name.

Miriam held her shawl close to her chest, her fingers tight around the edge as if it could protect her from her own story. Rehan stood beside her, his face a quiet mixture of worry and love.

He was the first to speak. His voice trembled. "Doctor… when we're together, just before she… reaches that moment, her body starts to shake. She collapses. For a few seconds, she doesn't move at all. Her eyes close. I think she's gone. Then suddenly—she wakes up."

Miriam lowered her eyes. Her silence was not empty; it was heavy, full of fear she could barely hold. "When it happens," she whispered, "I lose myself. My body jerks. I faint. And when I wake, I feel drained and ashamed. I'm afraid of that moment now. Afraid of what love might do to me."

The air in the room felt still, charged — like the moment before a storm breaks. What they thought was danger was, in truth, a whisper from the brain's secret world — an ancient rhythm gone astray.

The Hidden Lightning

Orgasm — that fleeting, blinding moment of joy — is not just the body's dance. It is the brain's orchestra, a surge of electric fire across its deepest networks.

The **temporal lobe**, **insula**, and **limbic system** — these are the regions where emotion, memory, and desire intertwine. They pulse together when the body reaches its peak.

In Miriam's brain, something small had gone awry — perhaps a hidden scar, or a tiny cluster of nerve cells that had always been too sensitive. It lay quiet for years, waiting. Until one day, love struck the right note.

As pleasure bloomed, her brain lit up like a city seen from the sky — dopamine, serotonin, oxytocin rushing through every neural street. But somewhere in that electric tide, the current slipped. A spark jumped where it shouldn't.

What should have been a wave of ecstasy became a storm — a **seizure** born from the right temporal lobe, the same place where mystics once claimed to hear the voice of God or feel themselves drift beyond the body.

Her body shook not from passion, but from a sudden burst of uncontrolled electricity — a thunderclap hidden within desire.

The Myth of Control

Love is tender, but it is also unpredictable. Sometimes it opens doors we never knew existed inside us.

Rehan, a man of logic, sat beside Miriam's bed when we admitted her for observation. His fingers never left hers. He looked like someone trying to protect a flame in a storm.

Through the night, we watched her brain on the EEG — a pattern of light and shadow across the screen. When she was shown gentle, romantic stimuli, the lines suddenly spiked.

There it was — **orgasm-induced epilepsy**, a condition so rare that only a handful of cases had ever been described. Two-thirds of those affected are women. The seizures often begin in the right temporal lobe — the brain's gate to emotion, memory, and transcendence.

Some patients say that, in those moments, they feel as though they are floating, leaving their bodies, hearing sounds that no one else can hear. For others, it's just a blank space followed by exhaustion and confusion.

The Quiet after the Storm

The next morning, when Miriam woke, the room was filled with soft light. She looked at me, her eyes asking the question she could not speak.

"This isn't madness," I told her gently. "It isn't weakness. It's your brain — a small part of it firing at the wrong time. We can calm it. You will live normally again. You don't have to be afraid of love."

Rehan's shoulders finally relaxed. Miriam's hands, which had been clenched for so long, opened slowly — like a flower relearning sunlight.

Outside, the world moved on, unaware that inside this small room, a mystery had found its name — where pleasure became lightning, and lightning learned to rest.

29

Unstoppable Laughter

It began, as strange things often do, on a day that felt perfectly ordinary.
The headmistress stood in my doorway, her umbrella dripping a small dark circle onto the tiles. Her face was composed, but her voice trembled faintly.

"It's about Arthur," she said. "He's such a gentle child… but something happens to him in class. I don't know what it is."

Arthur was ten. A quiet boy with curls that fell into his eyes. He loved his notebooks, the smell of new pencils, the soft hum of the ceiling fan.

Until the laughter came.

It began as a small twitch at the corner of his mouth. Then a sound escaped — quick, strange, and bright. Another followed, and another, until it filled the room. At first, the children laughed with him. Then they stopped. There was something in it that didn't belong — hollow, sharp, and unsettling.

If you looked closely, you'd see that Arthur's eyes weren't laughing. They were distant, as though his mind had gone somewhere far away.

"Arthur," his teacher whispered, "what's funny?"

He couldn't answer. The laughter kept pouring out until it stopped on its own. He sat still, breathing hard, pale and shaken, as if waking from a place he didn't remember visiting.

At home, it frightened them even more.

"He laughs at the worst times," his mother told me. Her fingers clutched the edge of her shawl. "Once, during his grandfather's prayer, he started laughing. He couldn't stop. Then he began to cry."

Her eyes glistened. "At first, we thought he was being cruel. But afterward, he looks lost. Like he's been somewhere and can't find his way back."

When Arthur came to see me, the afternoon light rested gently on his face. He sat on the edge of the chair, his feet not touching the floor. His small hands gripped the sides, as if holding himself steady against something unseen.

"Arthur," I asked softly, "when the laughter comes, what do you feel?"

He blinked, thought for a moment, then whispered, "Nothing. I don't even know it's happening."

That word — *nothing* — hung heavy in the air.

I turned to his parents. "Arthur isn't laughing because he wants to," I said quietly. "It's not mischief. It's not joy. It's something called *gelastic epilepsy*."

They listened, still and silent, as I explained.

"Gelastic seizures are rare," I told them. "The word *gelastic* comes from the Greek *gelos*, which means laughter. These seizures cause sudden bursts of laughter or giggling — laughter that comes at the wrong time, and without happiness behind it. It's not the laughter of joy. It's the laughter of confusion."

I watched their faces, saw both relief and sorrow stirring together.

"These episodes," I continued, "are true epileptic seizures — moments when the brain releases sudden bursts of electricity. During them, the person has no control, no awareness. Sometimes there's a blank stare, or small movements they don't realize they're making — fidgeting, lip-smacking, even the laughter turning suddenly into tears. When that happens, it's called a *dacrystic seizure*."

Arthur's mother held her breath.

"Where in the brain does it come from?" his father asked quietly.

"Usually," I said, "it begins deep inside, in a small part called the hypothalamus — the place that helps us feel emotions. Sometimes there's a tiny, harmless growth there, called a *hypothalamic hamartoma.* It's not cancer, but it can send the wrong signals, and those signals come out as laughter."

They looked at Arthur, sitting small and quiet in his chair, his curls shining in the light.

"The laughter," I said softly, "isn't joy. It's electricity."

His mother's lips trembled. "So he's not mocking us?"

"No," I said. "Not at all. Just as some children need glasses to help their eyes see clearly, Arthur's brain needs help finding its calm. The laughter isn't defiance — it's the brain's way of crying out."

For a long time, none of us spoke. Only the ceiling fan hummed, steady and low.

In the weeks that followed, we spoke to his teachers, his classmates. Slowly, the fear began to fade. The cruel nickname — *Laughter Boy* — disappeared from the hallways. The other children began to understand.

And when Arthur left my room one evening, holding his mother's hand, the light outside had turned gold — soft and forgiving. At the door, she looked back once. Her eyes were tired, but they carried something new: the quiet peace that comes when a mystery finally has a name.

Outside, a bird called from the neem tree. And somewhere, faint but still present, the memory of laughter lingered — fragile, human, and strangely tender.

30

Shout and Make Him Fall

Dr. Mehta still remembers that day — not as an image, but as a sound.
A door closing softly. The hum of the ceiling fan. And beneath it all, the trembling silence of a man afraid of his own body.

He was twenty-five. Japanese. Impeccably polite, his voice so gentle it could be mistaken for calm. Yet there was something fragile in the way his hands rested on his knees — as if he were trying to keep the air around him still.

"Doctor," he began, his tone barely rising above a whisper, "when someone shouts near me, I… collapse."

He paused, searching for words that could hold his shame. "It doesn't have to be anger. Just a raised voice. Even from far away — my body goes cold, I start shaking, and then… I fall. I don't even remember falling."

His wife sat beside him, her worry quiet but constant. "Once," she said, "the neighbors were arguing outside. Before I could close the window, he was already on the floor." Her voice broke on the last word.

Dr. Mehta had seen many strange epilepsies — flashes of light that could summon storms in the brain, songs that could trigger collapse — but never one awakened by sound alone. Yet here was a man whose body obeyed the world's noise as if it were a command.

Tests followed — scans, EEGs, long hours under the low hum of machines. Everything appeared ordinary until they played a simple recording of a man shouting.

The change was immediate. A shiver ran through him. His eyes flickered, his muscles tightened, and then — his body folded in on itself as though the sound had reached inside and pulled a hidden wire.

The test was stopped at once. Silence filled the room, heavy and waiting. When the young man opened his eyes again, confusion blurred his face. Then came the guilt.

"Am I cursed?" he whispered. "Or broken? It feels like my body betrays me — like I'm being punished for something I don't remember."

The doctor shook his head. "No," he said softly. "You're not cursed. Your brain is simply too sensitive to sound. The part that listens — the temporal lobe — reacts to loud voices as if they were physical blows. It's a condition called *reflex epilepsy*. Rare, but real."

He leaned forward and spoke gently, as if explaining something sacred.

"Reflex epilepsy is a special kind of epilepsy," he said, "where seizures don't appear out of nowhere — they're triggered. Every time the person meets a certain sound, sight, or thought, the brain reacts the same way. The trigger is consistent, like a switch that always turns on the storm."

The man listened carefully, his eyes fixed on the doctor's hands as they moved in calm gestures.

"Triggers can be almost anything," The doctor continued. "Flashing lights, particular patterns or colors, sudden noises — even a song, a word, or a touch. Some people experience seizures when they read, calculate, or even enter water. Each brain finds its own fragile spot."

He paused, letting the words settle.

"In your case, it's sound. When someone shouts, your brain receives a rush of signals — too many, too fast. The neurons in the hearing center fire all at once, like sparks leaping through a wire. That sudden flood of electricity overwhelms the system, and your body shuts down for a moment. You don't faint — you seize. For you, a raised voice isn't just noise. It's electricity."

The man's eyes filled. "So… it's not the anger that hurts me. It's the sound of it."

"Yes," doctor said. "You're not afraid of people. You're reacting to the world's volume."

Outside, the hospital murmured with life — car horns, vendors, televisions, voices rising and falling like tides. But for that young man, the city itself had become a storm. Every sound carried the chance of lightning.

So the medical team built him a plan — one of quiet and gentleness. He would learn to live in calm:

- avoiding sudden noises and heated arguments,
- using soft music and slow speech as medicine,
- exploring treatments that soothe the brain — vagal nerve stimulation, special diets that steady its rhythm,
- and, most of all, finding safety in understanding rather than fear.

For the first time, the man smiled. It was a small smile, fragile but real.

As he and his wife left the clinic, their footsteps echoed softly down the corridor. A nurse laughed somewhere in the distance, and for a moment, he flinched. Then he exhaled. The sound passed like a cloud.

Somewhere deep in his mind, the storm still waited — silent, listening. But that day, it had a name. And names, could turn fear into light.

31

Toothbrush Strikes You Down

Dr. Micheal often said that the strangest illnesses wear the most ordinary faces. Anita's face was one of them — young, radiant, and full of life. At nineteen, she had plans, laughter, and a future so bright that even her mother's scolding couldn't dim it. Every morning began the same: sunlight pouring through the window, a song on the radio, the soft rasp of her toothbrush against her teeth.

Until one morning, she didn't get up.

Her mother remembered the sound — the brush falling, the water still running. She ran to the bathroom to find Anita on the floor, trembling. The toothbrush lay beside her, the foam from the toothpaste spreading like a small, white sea.

"Doctor," her mother said later, her voice shaking, "it happens every time she brushes. Her body stiffens. She falls. Now we make her sit while brushing, but… it still happens."

Doctor looked up. "Only when brushing?" "Yes," the mother whispered. "It's not fear or fainting. It's like her body forgets how to stay awake."

Anita sat beside her, fragile and silent. "Doctor," she said softly, "when I brush my teeth, I see a flash of light — like lightning behind my eyes. Then I can't move. Everything stops. I just… fall."

Doctor nodded slowly. Her words were too precise to ignore. He had heard of rare forms of reflex epilepsy — triggered by music, touch, even sight. But this… this was different.

During testing, Anita held the brush again, under the gentle hum of the EEG machine. The room was silent except for the faint rhythm of bristles against enamel. Then, suddenly, the machine spiked — sharp lines, like a scream on paper. Her body went rigid, her eyes distant, her small frame trembling.

The test was stopped abruptly. When she came to, she looked terrified — not of dying, but of living with something she didn't understand.

He spoke gently. "Anita, what you have is called *toothbrushing epilepsy another form of Reflex Epilepsy*. It's rare — almost unheard of. When you brush, the rhythmic movement, the touch, maybe even the sound — it sends a signal your brain can't handle. It's like a short circuit."

Her mother clasped her hand. "So she can't brush her teeth anymore?"

Dr. Micheal smiled faintly. "She can. We'll just change how. Use a softer brush. Move slowly. Take breaks. The medicine will help too."

Weeks later, Anita began brushing again — carefully, quietly. Her mornings were no longer careless, but they were hers once more. Each motion was a small act of courage — a defiance against the strange betrayal of her own brain.

And somewhere, far away, another man — forty-two years old — had once fallen to the same rhythm, only to rise again with treatment and time.

Toothbrushing epilepsy remains one of medicine's rarest whispers — a reflex seizure where the simple act of brushing one's teeth can awaken a storm of electric chaos in the brain. It begins within seconds — with twitching, stiffness, or a fall — born from a surge in the brain's sensory and motor regions.

Through tests like EEG, doctors can trace the storm's path, and with care — gentle brushing, altered habits, and anti-seizure medication — they can calm it.

32

The Fatal Ringtone

Dr. Justin Andrews still remembers her name — **Ayana** — a young nurse of Apache descent who worked at the Cleveland Clinic. She was known for her calm voice, her soft laughter, and the quiet strength that made patients trust her instantly.

But one morning, that same world of sound she loved turned against her. They brought her into the emergency room on a stretcher — body convulsing, breath shallow, eyes rolled upward. Monitors screamed in alarm. For a moment, even the seasoned doctors stood frozen.

When Ayana finally regained consciousness two days later, her voice was barely a whisper. "Doctor… did I die?" Dr. Andrews leaned close. "No, Ayana. But you came very close."

Her eyes filled with confusion, then fear. "It was the sound again," she murmured.

"What sound?" She hesitated. "The ringtone… the Marimba one — from the iPhone. Every time I hear it, something happens. My whole body locks up. I can't move. Then… everything disappears."

Her colleagues later confirmed it. "It's real, Doctor. If that ringtone plays anywhere — from a patient's phone, or down the hall — she freezes, then collapses. We thought it was nerves. Until she stopped breathing one day."

It sounded impossible — until the tests began. During EEG monitoring, the doctors played a few soft tones — nothing happened. But when they played that familiar Marimba ringtone, the screen erupted with electrical storms. Her temporal lobe — the part of the brain that processes sound and emotion — went into chaos. Within seconds, Ayana's body stiffened, her hands trembled, and the seizure began.

They stopped the sound immediately. When she awoke, Dr. Andrews explained it gently. "Ayana, what you have is something called musicogenic epilepsy. Your brain isn't reacting to the music itself — it's reacting to the rhythm and pattern of sound. For most people, it's harmless. But for you, it's like lightning."

Her parents, sitting in silence, looked stricken. "Is this a curse?" her mother asked softly. Dr. Andrews shook his head. "Not a curse — just a storm that begins inside."

The hospital soon issued a notice: **"The iPhone Marimba ringtone is banned within hospital premises."** Posters appeared near the wards: **PLEASE CHANGE YOUR RINGTONE.**

And from that day onward, no one dared play that melody again. Ayana recovered slowly. She kept her phone forever on silent.

When Dr. Andres asked her why, she smiled faintly and said, "Silence saved my life once, Doctor. I trust it more than music now."

Sometimes, even the gentlest sound can awaken the fiercest storm. And in Ayana's case, a simple ringtone almost claimed her life.

33

People Hate Me

He entered my office like a shadow unsure of its place in the light — nineteen, tall, and trembling with the quiet shame of someone who no longer believed he deserved to be seen. His father followed behind him, shoulders heavy, eyes that had forgotten how to rest.

"Doctor," the father began, his voice soft, "my son hasn't gone to school for months. He refuses to meet friends or relatives. He says… people feel uncomfortable just by looking at him."

The boy — Haruto — sat down carefully, as if afraid even the chair might disapprove of him.

"Haruto," I said gently, "this room is safe. No one will judge you here. Tell me what happens."

He hesitated, then spoke in a whisper that barely belonged to him. "My classmates avoid sitting near me. I think my breath smells bad. My face feels strange — unpleasant. My voice sounds wrong. I can tell people are upset when I'm around. Even strangers on the street… I can feel their discomfort."

His father looked away. The room fell silent, filled only by the soft hum of the air conditioner and the unspoken ache between them.

I leaned forward. "Haruto," I said softly, "what if I told you something? It's not the world that feels uneasy around you. It's your mind — it's tricking you into believing you're a burden."

He looked up at me, startled, his eyes wide like someone hearing his own name after a long time.

"This feeling you carry," I continued, "has a name. In Japan, it's called *Taijin Kyofusho.* It means the fear of offending others — a deep worry that your presence, your gaze, your words might disturb someone. It's not pride, and it's not weakness. It's a kind of empathy that has turned inward, eating itself."

Taijin Kyofusho is a rare form of social anxiety — not about being *judged*, but about *causing pain.* Those who suffer from it often blush, tremble, avoid eye contact, or isolate themselves, terrified that even their breath or expression could upset someone. In a culture that prizes harmony and respect, it is empathy twisted into torment — the heart's politeness turned into a prison.

I told him, "You don't have bad breath, Haruto. You don't have an ugly face or a broken voice. What's hurting you is not your reflection — it's your belief that you don't deserve to take up space."

He said nothing, but his eyes softened — just a little.

Weeks passed. He came for therapy regularly. First, he stopped waiting by the door and began sitting among the other patients. Then, one morning, he smiled when I greeted him.

And one day, almost shyly, he said, "Doctor… I went to the park yesterday. There were people around. I thought they would stare. But they didn't."

I smiled. "That's because, Haruto, the cruelest eyes were never theirs — they were yours."

He nodded, quietly. The fog inside him was beginning to lift. Not gone, but thinning. In Japan, where silence is kindness and politeness is sacred, some hearts break not from rejection, but from imagining they cause it.

"The greatest prison people live in is the fear of what others think." — *David Icke*

34

Those Who Loved the Victim

"Sometimes, mercy arrives like an intruder — uninvited, but impossible to drive away."

He was thirty-two, built like a soldier, dressed like a gentleman. His name was Daniel. When he sat across from me that morning, I could see the fatigue in his eyes — not the kind that comes from lack of sleep, but from living too long inside a war between duty and conscience.

He had been part of a kidnapping ring — trained, efficient, and disturbingly calm. The kind of man who could plan a crime with surgical precision, then eat dinner as if nothing had happened. But something *had* happened. Something had cracked the surface of that coldness, letting the light in.

"I don't know what came over me, Doctor," he said. His voice was steady, but his fingers trembled slightly. "I've never been the emotional type. But that day… something broke."

I waited. Silence has a way of loosening memories.

He began again, slower now, almost whispering. "We only targeted the wealthy. Never hurt anyone. Just business — clean, fast, controlled. Twenty-five jobs, no mistakes."

He looked away, his throat tightening. "But the last one was different."

"How so?" I asked gently.

"The man we took — he was about fifty. When we locked him in that room, he kept holding a photo. A little girl. Maybe ten years old. I asked who she was. He said, 'My daughter.'" He swallowed hard. "She looked like my sister. The one I lost years ago."

The memory seemed to hollow him out. His next words came out like confession. "He asked if I had children. I said no. But that question… it didn't leave me. I started seeing him as a father, not a target. I brought him real food. We talked. He told me about his music, his wife, how he missed the morning sun on his porch. One night, we even shared a drink."

He paused. "And then I did something I can't explain."

I leaned forward. "What did you do, Daniel?"

He looked up, eyes wet but proud. "I let him go. I told him to run before the others came back. He didn't even look back. A few days later, they caught me."

No self-pity. No heroism. Just quiet guilt — the kind that hums long after the sirens fade.

"You broke your own code," I said softly. "You stopped seeing him as a hostage and started seeing him as human."

He nodded. "Yes, Doctor. I betrayed my brothers… but I couldn't betray myself."

I told him what he had experienced had a name — Lima Syndrome. It's the mirror image of Stockholm Syndrome: instead of the captive loving the captor, the captor grows compassion for the captive.

His eyes flickered with disbelief. "So I wasn't weak?"

"No," I said. "You were *awake*. You saw what others refuse to see — that even in darkness, the heart remembers how to feel."

He exhaled, shoulders loosening, as if forgiveness had finally found him.

After he left, I sat alone in the fading afternoon light, thinking of that moment — the quiet rebellion of kindness.

Years ago, during the 1996 Japanese embassy siege in Lima, Peru, a group of armed rebels had taken hundreds hostage. But as days turned to weeks, something strange happened: the captors began to care. They shared food, talked with their prisoners, even released some without reason. Compassion had infiltrated the ranks like a ghost — invisible, unstoppable.

Daniel's story was not so different. It was a reminder that cruelty, no matter how disciplined, can fracture under the smallest gesture of empathy.

35

Semen loss and death?

"What we fear most is often not death — but the stories we tell ourselves about it."

He was only fourteen — a thin, nervous boy from a quiet village in Kerala. His name was Sunil, and when he entered my room that morning, he looked as though he'd seen a ghost that only he could feel inside his body.

He sat down slowly, eyes darting to the corners of the room, as if someone might overhear what he was about to confess. His hands trembled.

"Doctor," he whispered, "I think I'm dying." I leaned closer. "Why do you feel that way, Sunil?"

He hesitated, then said, "Every night I have dreams… and then… it happens. I wake up and—" He stopped, his face burning. "It comes out. My pastor said it's dangerous. He said I'm losing my life energy. That men who waste it grow weak… and die." The room went still. Outside, the ceiling fan hummed softly.

"You mean semen?" I asked gently. He nodded, ashamed. "Yes. And sometimes… when I used to touch myself. I stopped doing it, but now it happens on its own. My yoga teacher said every drop of that energy could make a man strong — that it turns into blood, bones, and power. He said if I lose it, I lose everything."

Tears filled his eyes. "Doctor, look at me. My face has no glow. My memory is fading. I can't study. I think I'll die before twenty."

He believed every word. The terror in him was real — not of sickness, but of *sin.*

"Sunil," I said softly, "you're not dying. What you have is fear — not a disease. You've heard so many lies that your mind has begun to echo them as truth."

He looked uncertain, as though hope itself might betray him. "But… semen is life, isn't it?"

I smiled faintly. "So is breath. So is sweat. Your body releases what it doesn't need — every day. When you cry, do you lose your soul? When you bleed, do you lose your future? Of course not. Nature knows what it's doing. You are alive, healthy, and normal."

He stared at me in silence. "So… I'm not unclean?"

"Not even close," I said. "What's unclean is the guilt you've been taught to carry. Let that go. The heaviest thing in your body isn't semen — it's shame."

Weeks passed. Sunil began to eat again, to laugh softly when he spoke. The dark rings under his eyes faded. The glow he thought he'd lost had never left him — it was just hidden under fear.

A few months later, another patient came — Meera, twenty-one, a college student, sitting beside her mother. Her fingers twisted her scarf as she spoke.

"Doctor," she whispered, "I think I'm impure. I keep having a white discharge. My friends say it's a disease — that it's draining my strength, that no one will marry me."

Her eyes were wide with quiet shame — the kind passed down like an heirloom.

"How long have you noticed it?" I asked.

"Almost a year. I feel weak. Everyone says it means my body's losing its energy."

I smiled gently. "Meera, what you're describing is normal. Every woman has that discharge — it's how the body keeps itself clean. You're not losing life, you're *living* it. What's making you weak isn't your body — it's fear."

She blinked. "Fear?"

"Yes," I said. "Fear drains the body faster than any illness. And guilt is a poison that pretends to be virtue."

Over the next few weeks, Meera began to walk differently — lighter, freer. The anxiety that had lived in her spine slowly melted away.

Dhat Syndrome, found across South Asia, is not truly a disease — it's a story told too often, until it becomes real inside the mind. A tale that turns biology into blasphemy.

It teaches us something profound: that sometimes, the body doesn't need medicine — it needs permission to be itself.

36

The Scary Paris City

He sat before me in a silence that felt heavier than words — Professor Akio, a mild-mannered scholar from Japan whose life had been stitched together by books, music, and quiet reverence for beauty. But that day, his eyes were unfocused, almost haunted, as though they had seen something too beautiful to be real — or too real to be beautiful.

"Doctor," he began softly, "I just returned from Paris."

His voice trembled as he spoke the word — *Paris* — as if naming a ghost. "It was supposed to be the dream of my life. I studied French literature, read Hugo, Balzac, Baudelaire. I imagined the smell of rain on cobblestones, the music of café chatter, the river glowing under the evening light. For years, I kept that image alive inside me — a promise I made to myself. But when I finally stood there…"

He paused, his hands tightening on his knees. "It wasn't the Paris I knew. The streets were loud, the people hurried, impatient. Some laughed when I mispronounced a word. The waiters were cold. Everything felt… hollow. The city that once lived inside me — it shattered."

He looked at the floor, his voice shrinking. "I couldn't sleep. My heart raced for no reason. I wandered aimlessly, terrified by my own disappointment. I felt… betrayed. By a city."

I let the silence linger before speaking. "Akio, what you're describing is something rare — something we call *Paris Syndrome.* It happens when the dream of a place becomes larger than life, and the real world fails to match it. The shock doesn't just wound the mind — it confuses the soul."

He frowned slightly. "So this is… an illness?"

"Not an illness," I said. "A heartbreak — a collision between beauty imagined and beauty found. When you've loved a dream for too long, reality can feel cruel."

A small, fragile smile appeared on his face. "Maybe I fell in love with an illusion."

"Maybe," I said quietly. "But illusions are born from hope. And hope, even when it hurts, is still a beautiful thing."

Weeks later, Akio returned. The shadows under his eyes had softened. "Doctor," he said, "I think I understand now. The Paris I dreamed of belongs to poetry. The one I saw belongs to life. They are both real — just not the same."

I smiled. "And perhaps both are worth loving — the dream and the truth."

He nodded, his voice steady. "Yes. I think I'll go back someday. But this time, I'll meet the real Paris — not the one I invented."

Paris Syndrome reminds us that disappointment is not madness — it's the ache of awakening. It happens when beauty, stripped of fantasy, stands before us in its raw, imperfect truth.

"Expectation is the root of all heartache." — William Shakespeare

37

Beauty That Breaks the Heart

Samantha was a young artist of Romanian origin — a woman who painted silence, color, and emotion with the same delicate precision. Her dream had always been to see Italy, the land of Michelangelo and Da Vinci.

When she finally arrived, she wrote to me later, "Doctor, something strange began to happen in Florence."

She had gone there with a group of friends — first to see the Vatican in Rome, but someone suggested, *"Let's begin with Florence — the city of the Renaissance."*

From the moment she stepped onto its cobblestone streets, she said, "it was as if the city was whispering."

I asked her, "What happened, Samantha?"

She took a deep breath. "It started in the Uffizi Gallery. I was standing before Botticelli's *Birth of Venus.* At first, I was enchanted like everyone else… and then suddenly my heart began to race. My palms were sweating. My chest tightened. Tears filled my eyes, and then everything went dark. I fainted."

"When I woke up in the hospital, the doctor said I was fine. But it happened again — twice. Once when I saw Michelangelo's *David.* Another time, when I stood before Da Vinci's sketches. It's hard to explain, Doctor… I wasn't scared. I was overwhelmed. It was too much beauty for one heart to hold."

Her voice trembled slightly. "I think Florence broke me a little… or maybe it opened me too much."

I smiled gently. "Samantha, what you experienced is known as *Stendhal Syndrome.* It happens when the mind and senses are flooded by beauty — so deeply that the body reacts as if it cannot contain it. Florence has witnessed this often. You are not alone."

She looked at me anxiously. "So… I'm not going mad?"

"Not at all," I said. "You are simply someone who feels deeply. When beauty moves us beyond what words can hold, our hearts protest. That's not illness, Samantha. That's humanity."

I told her, "Next time, take it slowly. Don't try to absorb too much in one day. When you feel overwhelmed, breathe deeply, sip some water, or eat a piece of chocolate. Let the moment pass through you instead of holding on to it."

She nodded.

A year later, she returned to see me. Her face carried a quiet radiance.

"Doctor," she said with a soft laugh, "I went to the Louvre in Paris this time. When I stood before *The Winged Victory of Samothrace,* I felt it coming again — that rush. But I remembered your words. I breathed slowly, ate a bit of chocolate, and waited. The feeling faded. I could finally look… and truly see."

I smiled. "Good. You didn't fight the feeling. You befriended it."

Stendhal Syndrome

Stendhal Syndrome is a rare psychosomatic condition that occurs when a person is overwhelmed by the beauty of art, nature, or profound experiences — so intensely that it causes physical and emotional symptoms.

People affected may experience dizziness, rapid heartbeat, fainting, confusion, anxiety, or even hallucinations when exposed to something extraordinarily beautiful — such as a masterpiece in a museum, a breathtaking cathedral, or a stunning landscape.

The syndrome is named after the 19th-century French writer Stendhal (Marie-Henri Beyle), who first described his own experience while visiting Florence's Basilica of Santa Croce in 1817.

He wrote that the beauty of the art and the history around him made his heart race and his mind spin — a mix of ecstasy and terror.

Doctors in Florence later documented similar reactions among art lovers visiting the city's galleries, leading to the term *Stendhal Syndrome.*

In essence, Stendhal Syndrome reveals how beauty itself can be overwhelming — too powerful for the mind to contain. It shows that art doesn't just move us emotionally; sometimes, it can unravel us completely, reminding us how fragile and sensitive the human heart can be in the presence of wonder.

38

The Rebel Within

Roger was a 58-year-old government officer — calm, polite, the sort of man who signed papers with precision and spoke only when needed. But the day he came to my clinic, he looked like someone haunted — not by another person, but by something inside himself.

His wife walked beside him, holding his left hand as one might hold the hand of a restless child.

"Doctor," she whispered, "you may not believe this… but Roger's hand doesn't belong to him anymore."

Roger's voice trembled. "It moves on its own," he said. "Last night, I was watching TV. Suddenly it snatched the remote and threw it away. Sometimes it unbuttons my shirt in public. Once… it tried to choke me."

Before I could respond, his left hand twitched, quick and sudden — like a flash of rebellion — and reached for my pen. Roger's right hand grabbed it instantly, pressing it down against the table.

"I have to hold it," he said quietly. "It doesn't listen."

His wife's eyes were wet. "He talks to it, Doctor," she said softly. "He tells it to behave, sometimes even ties it when he sleeps."

I leaned closer. "Roger, do you feel afraid of it?"

He nodded. "Yes. I'm terrified. It feels… alive. As if someone else is living inside my arm."

After a few tests, the truth began to unfold. Roger had suffered a mild stroke weeks earlier — one that had damaged the **corpus callosum**, the bridge that allows the two sides of the brain to speak to each other.

I explained gently, "Your left hand is still yours, Roger. But the part of your brain that helps both sides cooperate has been injured. Now, one side acts without permission from the other. It's not a spirit or a curse — it's confusion, born inside your own mind."

He looked at his hand for a long time, as if seeing it for the first time. "So I'm not losing my sanity?"

"No," I said. "Your mind is sound. It's just that your hand no longer waits for your command."

A faint smile appeared on his face. "Then I'll keep talking to it," he said. "Maybe it'll listen one day."

"That's good," I replied. "Sometimes kindness works better than control."

A month later, Roger returned. His wife was smiling this time. "It still moves," he admitted, "but I don't fight it anymore. I've learned to make peace with it. I think it understands me now."

I smiled. "You're not battling your hand anymore, Roger. You're teaching it to belong."

Alien Hand Syndrome is a rare and unsettling neurological condition in which a person's hand seems to act **with a will of its own**. The hand may move, grasp, or touch objects independently — without conscious intent — even opposing the actions of the other hand.

It often follows **damage to the brain's communication pathways**, especially the **corpus callosum**, **frontal lobe**, or **parietal lobe**. Strokes, brain surgery, trauma, or degenerative diseases like Creutzfeldt–Jakob can trigger it.

The syndrome arises when the brain's motor systems act without the conscious mind's awareness — a split between **intention and movement**, leaving the person feeling like a stranger inside their own body.

There's no complete cure, but **behavioral therapy**, **sensory feedback**, and **keeping the hand occupied** can help.

"The greatest battles are not fought on battlefields, but within our own minds."

39

Your Daughter Is a Stranger

The room was quiet when Reema walked in with her mother, Kamala. Reema was only twenty, bright-eyed, a promising paramedical student. Kamala, sixty-two, carried a calmness that didn't quite match the fear in her daughter's eyes.

Reema sat forward and whispered, almost pleading, "Doctor… my mother says I'm not her real daughter. She believes I'm an impostor—a copy of myself."

I turned to Kamala gently. "Why do you say this? What makes you feel she's not your daughter?"

Kamala looked straight at Reema, studying her face the way one studies a stranger in a crowd. "She looks exactly like my daughter," Kamala said slowly. "She talks like her. She moves like her. But I know she isn't her. Someone has taken my daughter away. This one,"—she pointed at Reema— "this is someone else. A perfect imitation. But not her."

Reema's voice cracked. "Amma… I've been with you every day. I've never left home except to study. I'm your daughter."

Kamala shook her head. "No. My daughter's eyes don't move like yours. Her face doesn't have this look. You're pretending. Don't try to fool me."

The air thickened with silence—the kind that doesn't just fill a room but presses down on it.

Kamala's words weren't cruelty. They were symptoms. She was showing a rare and haunting condition called Capgras syndrome—a disorder in which the mind recognizes the face but rejects the person. It convinces itself that someone close—a child, a partner, a parent—has been replaced by an identical impostor.

Kamala had suffered a stroke a few months earlier. The stroke had damaged the fragile bridge between her brain's *recognition center* and *emotion center*. She could see her daughter's face, but the warm, instinctive feeling of *"This is mine"* had vanished. Her brain, desperate to explain the void, spun a story that felt utterly real to her: her real daughter was gone, and this was a stranger wearing her face.

A month later, after therapy and medication, I asked Kamala softly, "How does your daughter feel to you now?" Kamala said, "She sounds like my daughter on the phone. But when I see her in person, it's not her. It's that other woman again."

Reema held her mother's hands tightly. She understood, but understanding doesn't soften the pain of being seen as a stranger by the person who raised you. "She asks me how she can trust the food I cook," Reema whispered. "Doctor, it's like losing her… while she's sitting right next to me."

Capgras Syndrome

Capgras Syndrome is a rare and fascinating psychological disorder in which a person believes that someone close to them — such as a spouse, parent, or friend — has been replaced by an identical **impostor**.

The affected person can recognize the familiar face but feels a strange emotional disconnection, as if something essential is missing. This mismatch between recognition and emotional response tricks the brain into believing, "This looks like my loved one… but it isn't them."

Capgras Syndrome often appears in people with **schizophrenia**, **dementia**, or after **brain injury**, especially to areas that link facial recognition with emotion (like the temporal and limbic regions).

It can be deeply distressing — both for the patient and for those they accuse of being "doubles." Treatment focuses on addressing the underlying condition, using **antipsychotic medication, therapy**, and **family support**.

40

The World-Famous Nose

She entered my office like someone walking into a storm — quiet, careful, afraid that even her footsteps might draw attention. Her scarf was wound tightly around her face, not as an ornament of modesty, but as armour — a fragile wall against unseen eyes.

Her name was Anya, a brilliant postgraduate student at one of the world's most respected universities. When she finally sat across from me, she hesitated, then began to unwind her scarf with trembling fingers.

"Doctor," she whispered, "look at my face."

I looked. And for a moment, I forgot to breathe. There was nothing wrong. Her features were striking, even graceful — the kind of symmetry painters chase for centuries. She was extraordinary beautiful.

But her eyes, full of panic, demanded an answer I could not give.

"Do you see it?" she asked. "My nose. It's huge… distorted. People stare. Some laugh. I know they do."

I looked again — searching for what she saw. But what she described existed only in her imagination, not in flesh and bone. Yet to her, it was real — unbearably real.

Every word, every gesture carried the weight of obsession. She hid her face from cameras, turned away from mirrors, and avoided friends who once adored her. Her world had shrunk to the size of her reflection — one she no longer trusted.

As she spoke, I was reminded of the Malayalam Novelist Vaikom Muhammad Basheer's haunting tale, *"The World-Famous Nose."* How a single idea — once planted — can twist itself around the mind until it replaces reality.

Eventually, the story came out. It began with a single comment, tossed carelessly one afternoon by her boyfriend: "I don't like her nose."

Six words — meaningless to him, but deadly to her. They didn't fade. They took root. They echoed in her mind long after his voice was gone. Now, years later, that casual remark had become her private ghost.

Anya was not vain. She was not delusional. She was suffering from Body Dysmorphic Disorder — a condition where the mirror turns cruel, and beauty becomes a battlefield between perception and truth.

I told her gently, "Your eyes see something that your mind has reshaped. It isn't your face that's changing, Anya — it's your belief."

She nodded, tears sliding down her cheeks. "Then how do I stop seeing it?" "It will take time," I said. "But the healing begins the moment you stop fighting the mirror — and start questioning it."

Over months of therapy and slow courage, Anya began to reclaim herself. One morning, she came without the scarf. She still avoided mirrors, but she smiled — a small, defiant smile — as if she'd finally realized that her face had never been her enemy.

Body Dysmorphic Syndrome

Body Dysmorphic Syndrome (or Body Dysmorphic Disorder, BDD) is a psychological condition where a person becomes deeply preoccupied with perceived flaws in their appearance — flaws that others cannot see. The distress can be so intense that it leads to isolation, anxiety, depression, and repeated cosmetic procedures that offer no relief.

The disorder stems from distorted visual and emotional processing in the brain, often linked to serotonin imbalance and obsessive–compulsive traits. Treatment involves cognitive-behavioral therapy (CBT) and selective serotonin reuptake inhibitors (SSRIs) —

helping patients rebuild a truthful, compassionate view of themselves.

"Sometimes, the monster isn't in the mirror. It's in the mind of the one who dares to look."

41

The Taste of Books

He entered my room not as a man, but as someone newly born into a strange world — curious, wide-eyed, untamed.

James was tall, broad-shouldered, the kind of man whose presence once filled a room with quiet command. Yet now, he moved like a child lost in a dream, clutching his wife's hand as if it were the last real thing left.

His other hand wandered. It drifted across my desk, tracing the curve of a pen, the chill of a glass paperweight, the smooth edge of a wooden frame. His fingers trembled with restless wonder, as though the world spoke to him through touch alone. Then, he lifted a book, brought it to his face, and whispered, "It smells… alive."

His wife gently took it from him, her eyes hollowed by sleepless nights.
"Doctor," she said softly, "this started after the surgery. He touches everything, smells them, licks them. Sometimes… he even tries to eat them. I can't take him anywhere anymore."

James reached for the glass of water and drank it all in one gulp — not from thirst, but as if testing the taste of reality itself.

"What are you thinking right now, James?" I asked.

He smiled faintly, eyes on the papers before him. "I'm hungry," he said. "Can I eat this?"

His wife's voice trembled. "He eats anything — plastic, cloth, even flowers. He hugs strangers in the street. Last week someone slapped him because he wouldn't let go."

It was hard to reconcile this gentle, wandering man with the soldier he once was — disciplined, precise, composed. Now he laughed at walls, stood in front of speeding cars, and said, "It's fine if they hit me. Why should I be afraid?"

When I told her the diagnosis — Klüver–Bucy Syndrome — she fell silent.

"It happens when both temporal lobes of the brain, especially the amygdala, are damaged," I explained quietly. "That part of the brain helps us recognize danger, feel fear, and understand what's safe or wrong. When it's injured, the mind loses its boundaries. People begin touching, tasting, or approaching things they shouldn't — not because they choose to, but because the compass inside their brain has broken."

She nodded slowly, as though trying to accept a map of a country she had never wanted to visit.

Later, in the scanning room, James ran his hand along the smooth curve of the MRI machine and murmured, "It's beautiful. I want to hug it." The technician looked away, unsure whether to smile or cry.

Klüver–Bucy Syndrome can follow head trauma, brain surgery, strokes, or viral infections like herpes simplex encephalitis. The damage cannot be undone — the missing pieces of the brain never grow back. But with medication, therapy, and patience, the storms can calm.

When I last saw them, his wife was holding his hand as he traced the fabric of her sleeve with wonder. Her eyes were tired, but steady. She didn't pull away.

In the quiet of my office that evening, I wrote his notes slowly. Klüver–Bucy Syndrome (KBS): a rare, fragile world where the mind forgets its fences.

It begins when both temporal lobes — especially the amygdala — are injured. The amygdala is the keeper of emotion, the gate that lets us feel fear, recognize danger, and draw meaning from what we see. When it is lost, the world itself becomes raw and borderless.

People with KBS live in that borderless world. Their emotions flatten; fear dissolves. They become placid, strangely calm — walking toward danger without hesitation. That is the first sign: **placidity**, the quiet loss of fear.

Then comes **hyperorality** — a restless need to explore everything by touch and taste. Objects no longer stay objects; they must be known through the mouth — keys, cloth, paper, flowers. To them, the world is texture and flavor.

There is also **hypersexuality** — an increase in desire without context or restraint — and **hypermetamorphosis,** a kind of visual hunger where every sight demands attention, every movement becomes irresistible. Even light, color, and motion call to them like whispers.

And finally, **changes in appetite** — an insatiable urge to eat, to chew, to consume even what cannot nourish. Sometimes, the hunger turns toward non-foods: coins, plastic, dirt.

These symptoms — fearlessness, hypersexuality, hyperorality, hypermetamorphosis, and compulsive eating — are the strange constellation by which KBS is known.

The syndrome was first described nearly a century ago, in the 1930s, when two scientists — Heinrich Klüver and Paul Bucy — removed parts of the temporal lobes in monkeys and watched their behavior transform. They became fearless, hypersexual, endlessly curious — creatures of sensation rather than understanding. What began as an experiment became a window into what happens when the emotional compass of the brain is broken.

In humans, KBS can follow head injuries, infections, strokes, or degenerative diseases like advanced Alzheimer's. Each cause erases a piece of the emotional map, until the person left behind wanders through the world guided only by impulse and wonder.

For James, that wonder was both curse and innocence. He was not lost in madness — only unmoored from fear.

As his wife once told me, "He sees beauty in everything now. Even in danger."

And perhaps that was true. For in the end, as he traced the edge of her sleeve with trembling fingers, there was peace in his face — a childlike awe that no damage could quite erase.

42

The Disobedient Left Hand

He arrived like a man constructed entirely of sharp edges—his collar crisp, every motion measured. Yet beneath that surface of perfect control, something fragile trembled, like glass beneath a steady hand.

Roshan sat down, his right hand gripping his left wrist as though restraining a secret that might escape.

"Doctor," he whispered finally, his voice dry and careful, "this hand… it isn't mine."

I almost smiled, thinking he was speaking in metaphor. But then I saw the way he watched it—with the cautious dread of someone observing a living thing that could betray him. His left hand lay perfectly still, but his eyes refused to trust it.

"When I try to write, or eat, or drive," he said, "it feels wrong. Like I'm using something borrowed that doesn't obey. It just… doesn't belong."
He gave a small, exhausted laugh. "It's like wearing a stranger's skin."

Roshan was a teacher—measured, articulate, admired by students and colleagues alike. But behind that calm exterior lived a private torment.
"If I told anyone else," he said softly, "they'd call me mad. So I act normal. Every day. Every minute."

His voice dropped lower. "Sometimes, the urge is so strong I've held a knife. The only way to feel whole is to cut it away. But I can't."

His words fell into the silence like stones. The left hand twitched slightly, and the right hand gripped harder—as if to anchor something that was slipping away.

This was no madness. His thoughts were clear. His reason, intact. What had come undone was the invisible thread between body and self—the wordless certainty that tells us, *this is mine.*

"Roshan," I said gently, "your pain is real. The part of your brain that recognizes your body—the right parietal lobe—has lost its alignment. It's sending the wrong signal, telling you this hand is foreign. That's why it feels wrong, as if it doesn't belong to you. But there are ways to quiet that confusion. To help you find peace again."

He said nothing. But his shoulders eased a little. For the first time, he looked at his hand not with hatred, but with grief—like someone gazing at a loved one they no longer understand.

That night, I wrote about him. *Body Integrity Identity Disorder.*

A rare and deeply unsettling condition where identity and anatomy fall out of sync. People who live with it are certain—utterly certain—that a part of their body is not their own. They are not psychotic, and they do not wish to die. They long for alignment. They believe that by removing the unwanted limb, they will finally feel complete.

Their suffering comes not from pain, but from the presence of something that feels wrong—a mismatch between mind and flesh. Many describe it as a constant noise beneath the skin, an alien hum they can't silence.

The cause remains uncertain, but the right parietal lobe—the region that constructs the brain's internal body map—is often implicated. In scans, subtle differences sometimes appear there. The brain's image of the body no longer matches the physical truth, and the result is a haunting dissonance: a body that feels partly borrowed.

Because no ethical surgeon can amputate a healthy limb, most live in unbearable silence. A few, driven by desperation, attempt to do it themselves. It remains one of the most difficult questions in medicine—how to heal a disorder that exists between the physical and the existential.

Years ago, a surgeon in Scotland amputated the legs of two such patients. One later said, "That leg was never mine. I had to let it go." He found peace. The world found horror.

Medicine still stands divided—between duty and mercy, between the ethics of preservation and the compassion of understanding.

Roshan sat before me, his right hand still holding the left, but now with care rather than restraint.

"I'll try," he said quietly. "To live with it. Even if it never feels like it's mine."

He stood and left the room with a strange dignity.

And I thought—there is no stranger more terrifying, or more deserving of mercy, than the one who lives beneath your own skin.

43

Those Who Turn into Wolves

There are stories that seem to enter a room before the person does — stories that whisper in the air like an unseen wind. Freddie's story was one of them.

He walked in beside his mother — a tall, broad-shouldered man, but trembling inside like a child who had just woken from a nightmare. His eyes were ringed with sleepless nights, and his fingers twitched restlessly, curling as though they belonged to someone else.

"Doctor," his mother began softly, "he believes he's turning into a wolf."

Freddie's gaze flicked toward me, wild and pleading. His voice, low and uneven, carried the tremor of conviction. "Listen to me," he said. "My teeth are sharper now. My skin feels rougher. At night, when I hear them howl… I want to answer. The walls feel wrong. I don't belong here anymore. The forest is calling me home."

He wasn't acting. His fear was too real. There was a strange comfort in his madness — as if the thought of becoming a wolf gave him strength he had lost as a man.

"Freddie," I asked gently, "when you look in the mirror, what do you see?"

He hesitated, eyes flickering. "Not all of it yet. But my eyes are changing. My face too. Why won't anyone believe me?"

His mother's voice broke. "He scratches at doors at night, bites his own skin… He doesn't sleep anymore. He says wolves don't need rest."

I leaned closer. "Are you afraid of what's happening?"

He looked up — and for a moment, there was a smile, small and dangerous. "No. Wolves are strong. When I was human, people used me. They lied to me. They hurt me. Wolves don't get hurt."

And then came the truth — a confession whispered through the cracks of his voice, heavy with grief. A love that had rotted from within. His wife — the woman he had built his world around — had left him for a man of wealth and easy charm. The betrayal cut deep, deeper than words could reach, and the wound refused to close.

In the silence that followed, Freddie sought shelter where no one could touch him — in the flickering light of horror films. There, among the shadows and snarls, he found his kindred spirits — beasts and broken men tearing off their human masks. Somewhere in that darkness, he felt safe. Somewhere in those monsters, he found himself.

He was no longer Freddie the man. He became Freddie the wolf.

But this was no folklore, no curse of the moon. It was Clinical Lycanthropy — a rare psychiatric condition where a person truly believes they are transforming into an animal. Some howl, crawl, or refuse cooked food. Others see their reflection as something monstrous, no longer their own.

There are even rarer cases, like Boanthropy, where a person believes they are a cow or an ox — grazing, crawling on all fours, eating grass. In ancient times, such states were seen as curses from gods. The Bible speaks of King Nebuchadnezzar, who wandered like cattle in the fields — but today, we know these as delusional states born from trauma, psychosis, or brain dysfunction.

Freddie didn't need an exorcist. He needed healing. Therapy to separate the wolf from the man. Medication to calm the storm inside his mind. Love and patience to remind him of his humanness.

One evening, as the sessions drew on, he whispered, "I'm weak, Doctor… but the wolf in me is strong."

I smiled gently. "Then maybe it's time to teach the wolf to rest." Over time, the howling stopped. The eyes softened. And Freddie — fragile, human, and whole — began to return.

44

She Is Everywhere

The sky over Vancouver hung low that evening, pale and tired. Rain slid down the hospital windows in thin, trembling lines, like someone weeping behind glass. I held a cup of coffee from Tim Hortons, its warmth seeping into my palms, and watched the pavement outside shimmer under the yellow streetlights.

It was almost time to leave when Riana knocked on the door—softly, like someone afraid to disturb a fragile silence.

"Doctor Mathew," she whispered, "someone keeps calling. Three times now. He says he must see you tonight."

I looked up. "Didn't you tell him we're done for the day?"

"I did," she said, lowering her voice. "But he's downstairs. He won't leave." I sighed. "All right. Send him in."

Ten minutes later, a man walked in—a picture of order. Suit pressed. Collar stiff. Shoes polished so well they caught the light like mirrors. But beneath that perfect exterior was a quiet unease that filled the room.

His eyes flicked nervously toward Riana. "That's her," he whispered.

"Her?" I asked. "That's my secretary."

He didn't move. "You are Dr. Mathew, right?"

"Yes."

"Show me your ID."

His tone wasn't angry—it was frightened. The kind of fear that makes you double-check your own reflection. I showed him the card. His shoulders loosened slightly, but the dread stayed.

"Please don't think I'm insane," he said, leaning forward. "She's everywhere. She follows me. Sometimes she's my boss. Sometimes my wife. Sometimes my daughter. But it's always her. Always the same woman."

And there it was—the unmistakable sign of **Fregoli Delusion**.

Most patients with paranoia believe many are after them. But John—let's call him that—believed that one woman wore the faces of many.

"She started as a cashier," he said quietly. "I saw her at the supermarket. The way she smiled—it was Jenny's smile. My old girlfriend. When I drove away, I saw her again in my mirror. Same eyes. Same hands. Same way she touched her hair. That night, she was home before me… wearing my wife's face."

His voice trembled, not from madness—but from certainty.

"My wife says I'm imagining it. My mother prays for me. But I know it's her. Jenny. She's everywhere. She never leaves."

When I asked about Jenny, he hesitated. Then, like something long locked away, the truth began to spill.

There had been an accident years ago. He thought he had hit a child while reversing his car. He remembered seeing Jenny at the roadside, clutching a little girl. The guilt had stayed with him like an echo that never stopped.

In reality, there was no child. Only a fallen garbage bin. Jenny had not been there. She had moved on—married, with a family of her own. But John never did. Guilt took root, and slowly it began to twist itself into delusion.

Soon he began to see her everywhere—in strangers, in reflections, in every familiar smile. One face, infinite disguises.

With therapy, medication, and time, the spell began to lift. Jenny's face faded back into memory, where it had always belonged.

When John left my office months later, he paused at the door, as if expecting her to be standing there. There was no one. Only the rain, falling softly against the glass.

Fregoli Delusion is a rare psychiatric condition where a person believes that different people are, in truth, a single individual in disguise. It often appears in schizophrenia or after brain injury affecting the temporal lobe. Unlike Capgras syndrome—where familiar people seem replaced by impostors—Fregoli delusion convinces the mind that many strangers are one familiar soul wearing endless masks.

"Guilt is a quiet sculptor. If you let it, it will carve the same face into every shadow around you."

45

The Gas Chamber Inside

The hospital was quiet that evening. Rain tapped gently on the window glass, and the fluorescent lights hummed like a distant, restless thought. That's when Kim Yong walked into my office.

She was a 55-year-old Korean woman, small and fragile-looking, clutching her handbag to her chest as though it were the last safe thing in her world. Her daughter followed closely behind, eyes heavy with worry.

"Doctor," her daughter began softly, "they told us it's gas. But it's not. She can't sleep at night. She cries. She says her stomach is burning. Her chest feels like it's on fire."

I turned to Kim. "Tell me what's happening."

She kept her eyes low, as if the floor might judge her. Her hands trembled when she spoke. "Doctor… it starts here," she pressed her palm against her stomach. "It feels like gas building up, like a storm in a small room. Then it rises up to my chest. I can't breathe. My head hurts. It's like my body is trying to push something out—but nothing comes."

I asked quietly, "Does it happen when you're thinking of something?"

She nodded. "Yes. At night… the faces of those who hurt me come back. Every word they said. Every silence. I never said anything back. I never could."

Her daughter's voice broke in—a story spilling like water from a cracked jug.

For years, Kim had lived inside a prison of silence. Her first husband had treated her cruelly. His family, especially his mother, had sharpened their words like knives. She endured it all quietly. For the sake of her children. For survival.

Later, another man came—this time with gentle lies. He used her body, took her money, and left. She never told anyone. Not her friends. Not even her daughter. Her pain became invisible. But her body remembered.

Now, years later, that silence had turned into heat—burning in her chest and stomach. What doctors had dismissed as "gas" was something far deeper: Hwabyung.

Hwabyung is sometimes called "anger illness." It's a recognized cultural syndrome in Korea, more common in women who have swallowed pain for too long. The anger doesn't vanish. It hides in the body—burning, pressing, choking.

In therapy, Kim spoke softly at first. She had never learned to express anger. "In our home," she whispered, "good women don't talk back. We just… endure. If I spoke, they'd hate me. So I stayed quiet."

I looked at her gently. "But that silence is shouting inside you now, isn't it?"

Her eyes filled with tears. "Yes. My body remembers everything they did to me."

Week after week, Kim returned. Slowly, through psychotherapy, relaxation techniques, support from her daughter, and medication, the storm inside began to calm.

Two months later, I asked, "Kim, if you could speak to the people who hurt you, what would you say now?"

She lifted her head. Her voice trembled but did not break.

"You are doing wrong. I am not your slave. I have a mind, a body, and a soul. I am a woman made of marrow and flesh and feeling. I have a voice. And I should have spoken."

Her daughter wrapped her arms around her, crying.

For the first time, Kim smiled. A quiet, tired, beautiful smile. "Doctor," she said, "if the fire in me used to be a raging flame… now it's just warm tea. I can hold it. I can handle it."

And just like that, the gas chamber in her body began to open—not with a bang, but with the soft sigh of a woman finally allowed to speak.

"When pain is buried alive, it does not die. It turns into fire. But the moment you give it a voice… it becomes light."

46

Walking Corpse

The rain that evening didn't fall—it drifted, slow and uncertain, tracing delicate paths down the glass. Each drop seemed unsure where to go, like tears that had lost their reason. Inside the clinic, everything was still. The clock above the door ticked softly, patient and lonely.

That was when Arithra came in.

She moved like someone half-remembered by the world—thin, quiet, her presence barely disturbing the air. Her husband followed close behind, his face hollowed by sleepless nights.

She sat without looking up. He stood beside her, his hands twisting together.

"What brings you here, Arithra?" I asked.

Her reply was a whisper, fragile and cold. "Doctor… I'm dead."

For a moment, even the clock seemed to stop.

"Dead?" I repeated, gently.

She nodded. "I died two months ago. My heart stopped. What you see here—it isn't me. It's only what was left behind."

Her husband's voice broke. "She says she doesn't need food. That corpses don't eat. She stopped bathing, stopped speaking to anyone. She goes to the cemetery every morning and says her grave is waiting."

"Why would I eat?" she murmured. "A body without a soul doesn't feel hunger."

I leaned forward. "Arithra, I can see your pulse, your breath. You are alive."

Her eyes lifted to mine, distant and calm. "You're talking to a ghost, Doctor. My body moves, but I'm gone."

I chose my words carefully. "Arithra, your mind is suffering. There is an illness that can make people believe they are dead. It's called Cotard's Syndrome. When the brain sinks too deep into despair or trauma, it sometimes tries to escape the pain by erasing itself. It isn't death—it's sorrow pretending to be."

She frowned, a small crease between her brows. "So my brain is lying to me?"

"Yes," I said. "But lies can fade. You can return."

Her husband reached for her hand, trembling. "You're still here. You're my wife. Please, come back."

She turned toward him then. Something fragile passed through her gaze—a flicker of life, faint but true.

Time, medicine, and love slowly drew her back. Therapy. Soft evenings with her children. Quiet mornings filled with light. Piece by piece, she remembered the rhythm of being alive. Sometimes, she even laughed. But the ghost of that belief never vanished completely—it lingered, a shadow waiting by the door. And whenever it returned, her husband would take her hand, anchoring her again to the world of the living.

Months later, he came to see me alone. His eyes shone, though his smile was steady. "Doctor," he said softly, "it's like you gave me back my dead wife."

Cotard's Syndrome — sometimes called Walking Corpse Syndrome — is one of the strangest and rarest delusions known to medicine. Those who suffer from it believe, with unshakable certainty, that they are dead, that parts of them have vanished, or that nothing around them truly exists. Some even believe they are immortal—unable to die because they already have.

They stop eating, stop caring for their bodies, because why should the dead need sustenance?

It often grows from the deepest roots of depression or from damage to the fragile circuits of the brain that shape self-awareness.

It is a cruel, quiet illness—the kind that doesn't kill the body, only convinces it that it's already gone.

The cruelest illusion, after all, is not death. It's forgetting that you're still alive.

47

The Storm Inside you

Soria was sixty-five, a Cambodian woman who had lived through both war and memory. Montreal was her refuge now—a narrow street, a small apartment that always smelled of lemongrass, tea, and faint incense smoke. Yet inside her, another country still breathed. The past had not released her.

Her husband came first. A quiet man, his eyes carrying the exhaustion of someone who had seen too much. "Doctor," he said, his voice low and trembling, "please… you must see my wife."

When Soria walked in, she looked as if she'd been running from something no one else could see. She held her scarf close, her knuckles white.

"I thought I would die last night," she said. "The wind inside me—the KHAYAL KAAP—it came again. From my stomach to my head. My breath vanished. My heart stopped. I must have died."

Her husband placed a hand on her back. "You didn't die, Soria. You're here. You're safe." Then, turning to me, he said, "It happens at night. When she lies down, the wind rises. It rushes through her chest, into her head, and she faints. Back home, they say the head will burst. We call it KHAYAL KAAP."

KHAYAL KAAP—the wind attack. A belief born generations ago, still alive among those who carried Cambodia within them. They say the body holds sacred air, and when it escapes or rises too high, death follows.

I asked her softly, "Soria, what does it feel like when the wind begins?"

She pressed a hand to her chest. "It starts here. A pounding—like thunder trapped inside. Then it climbs. My neck, my head. My eyes feel they will burst. My hands go cold. My breath stops. And then… I faint. I know I am dying."

Her husband nodded. "We burn wicks, send the smoke toward her chest. We pull her legs so the wind can leave. Sometimes it helps."

Soria whispered, "Yes… sometimes the air escapes."

But what haunted her was not a spirit wind—it was panic. A sudden surge of the body's own alarm system. When the brain senses danger, it releases adrenaline. The heart races, the breath shortens, the chest tightens—all meant to save a life. But sometimes, the signal misfires. The body screams run even when there is no threat. That is a panic attack—terror without an enemy.

I told her gently, "Your heart feels as if it will stop, but it won't. The fear tricks your body into thinking you're dying. It's not the wind, Soria. It's the alarm—too sensitive, too loud."

She shook her head, eyes wet. "My cousin died like this. The wind took her."

Her husband added, "Everyone says so, doctor."

I explained, "Her heart may have truly failed. But your heart only races—it does not stop. What you feel is real, but it cannot kill you."

It took months of slow work—psychotherapy, medication, reassurance—for her to believe the storm inside her was not a curse, but her own body's mistaken cry for help.

And yet, whenever the wind rose outside her window, Soria would stop, press her chest, and whisper a prayer. Not out of fear—but out of memory.

"Sometimes, the ghosts we fear the most aren't the ones outside us—but the storms that rise within."

48

Enemies in your sleep

Let's call him Vinay Purohit.

Twenty-eight. Sharp, disciplined, the kind of man who could read the future through a spreadsheet. But when he walked into my office, something in him had cracked. His confidence was still there—polished on the surface—but behind it, I could see the tremor.

"Doctor," he said quietly, "I think I'm losing my mind."

He leaned forward, his voice trembling between logic and fear. "Every night, just as I start to fall asleep, I see things. I hear voices. They come when I'm halfway gone—and again when I'm waking up. It feels real. Too real."

I asked him to tell me what he saw.

He hesitated. Then, almost whispering, he said, "It begins when I lie down. The room goes still, and then something changes. A shadow appears. Once it was a man standing in the corner. Another night, I saw a spider—huge, the size of my hand—climbing the wall. Once, a woman's voice whispered, 'Aren't you coming?' And sometimes… I can't move. I try to scream, but nothing comes out. It feels like someone's pressing on my chest."

He looked at me, eyes pleading for an answer. "Doctor… are there ghosts here too? My mother thinks maybe someone cursed me. My old boss, perhaps. I left India too fast."

I smiled gently. "No, Vinay. What you're describing isn't a curse. It has a name—two, actually. Hypnagogic and hypnopompic hallucinations. They happen in that thin space between sleep and wakefulness. The brain starts dreaming before the body is fully asleep—or keeps dreaming after it's begun to wake."

He frowned. "So it's not real?"

"It feels real," I said. "That's what makes it terrifying. But it's the brain dreaming with its eyes open."

I explained that during those moments, the brain is still running on REM sleep—the same state where dreams are born. The muscles stay paralyzed, a built-in safety lock to keep us from acting out our dreams. But when the mind wakes too soon, you become trapped inside your own body—awake, but unable to move. The weight on the chest, the shadow, the whisper—it's all part of that frozen borderland.

It's called sleep paralysis. Frightening, yes. But harmless.

For the first time, Vinay exhaled. "Doctor, my job—it's brutal. I live on caffeine. I sleep three, maybe four hours. I'm never really off."

I nodded. "That's the perfect storm. Sleep too little, stress too much, and the wall between dreams and reality begins to thin. Your body begs for rest, but your mind won't stop. That's when the ghosts come."

He smiled faintly. "So half of me is asleep, half awake."

"Exactly," I said. "And in that half-light, the most rational mind can see impossible things."

Over the next few weeks, we worked quietly. Less caffeine. Regular sleep. A mild medication to steady his nights. His mother called from India; I told her her son wasn't cursed—just exhausted.

Soon, the voices fell silent. The spider never came back. The shadows faded into memory. When Vinay returned for his final visit, he looked rested—alive in a way he hadn't been before.

He grinned. "Doctor, the ghosts finally left."

I smiled. "They were never ghosts, Vinay. Just your mind asking for mercy."

49

The girl Who Couldn't Forget

Her name was **Harmeet Kaur**. She came with her brother, **Harpreet Singh** — a tall man whose presence felt like a shield against something no one else could see. His hands gripped the edge of her chair, steady and afraid to let go.

"Doctor," he began softly, "I don't even know if this is an illness. It just feels… wrong."

Harmeet sat beside him, calm but distant. Her fingers were laced so tightly they had turned pale. When she spoke, her voice carried the weight of too many sleepless nights.

"I remember everything," she said. "Every single thing. And I can't make it stop." I tried to lighten the moment. "That doesn't sound so bad. Most people wish they could remember more."

She shook her head slowly. "No. You don't understand."

Then, she began to describe a day — not an extraordinary one, just a forgotten Tuesday. But to her, it was alive. "It was the sixteenth of last month," she said. "I left home at ten sharp. At ten fifteen, I parked outside the McDonald's on Fraser Street. I ordered a vegetable sandwich, five dollars and fifty cents. The cashier's name was Ronia Wong — she gave me thirty cents change. It was drizzling. I wore a blue dress. I dried my hair with a blue towel in the car until eleven fifteen."

Her brother sighed. "That's what she does, Doctor. Every day, every memory. Even from when we were kids — she remembers the taste of the ice cream we had after her first tooth was pulled."

"Chocolate mint," Harmeet whispered, her eyes far away. Her memory wasn't sharp. It was relentless. When I asked what it felt like, she said, "It's like watching a movie that never ends. Every mistake, every loss, every moment I'd rather forget — they all stay. I can't pause it. I can't walk out of the theatre."

"Do you think it's a gift?" I asked.

She smiled faintly. "People think so. But there's no peace in remembering everything. My mind is full — like a cupboard that can't close. Even pain has nowhere to go."

What Harmeet lived with has a name **— hyperthymesia**, also known as **Highly Superior Autobiographical Memory**. It is a rare condition where the past refuses to fade. People like her can recall every day of their lives with absolute clarity — what they wore, what song played, how the air smelled. The memories arrive uninvited, bright and exact.

It isn't photographic memory. They can't recite books or numbers. They only remember their own story — every ordinary hour of it — in perfect detail.

For most of us, forgetting is mercy. It lets us keep walking forward. For Harmeet, that mercy was gone. Every hurt stayed sharp. Every goodbye stayed loud.

One evening, she looked at me and said quietly, "I wish there was a button. Just one. To erase a few days… enough to rest."

I told her, "Then let's find that button together."

No one fully understands why hyperthymesia happens. The answer seems to live somewhere in the folds of the brain — the amygdala, the hippocampus — the places where memory and emotion intertwine. In people like Harmeet, those regions burn brighter, as if the brain refuses to let the past dim.

There is no cure. But there can be quiet. Therapy, mindfulness, and medicine can help the flood slow down — not to erase, but to soften the edges, to let the past whisper instead of shout.

It took time — months of patience, learning how to live with the noise.
But one morning, she walked into my office smiling.

"Doctor," she said, "I still remember everything. But now, it doesn't hurt as much."

50

The Sleeping Attacker

He came in with his wife. **Robert** — tall, quiet, the kind of man who carries his guilt like a shadow. **Sylvie** — tense, voice brittle, as if fear had lived in her chest for too long.

They stood close, but not touching. The kind of closeness born not from comfort, but from survival.

Before I could speak, she did. "Doctor," she said, her voice trembling, "my husband tried to kill me… in his sleep."

Robert's head fell into his hands. "It's not what it sounds like. I don't remember it — any of it." He took a breath, his words shaking. "She says I hit her, kick her, shout. But I wake up with no memory. I swear, I'd never hurt her."

Sylvie's eyes filled with tears. "He's not lying. I've seen it. One night he punched the wall beside me. Another, he jumped up and threw the lamp across the room. Once…" — her voice broke — "he bit me."

Robert looked horrified. "In my dream, a dog was attacking me. I thought I was fighting it off."

She turned to me. "I don't sleep beside him anymore. I lock my door. Sometimes I hear him shouting names in the dark. What if he grabs something sharp?"

Robert's voice cracked. "I love her. But in my dreams, I'm someone else — a soldier, a stranger. My body believes it's real."

I'd seen this before — rare, unsettling, but unmistakable. "Robert," I said softly, "what you have is called **REM Sleep Behavior Disorder** — a condition where the body acts out dreams instead of keeping them locked away."

He looked up, confused.

"When we dream," I explained, "the brain usually shuts off our muscles, keeps us still. It's a kind of built-in safety. But in your case, that switch is broken. When you dream, your body doesn't stay still — it follows."

Sylvie's shoulders eased a little. "So it's not his fault?"

"No," I said. "His body just forgets it's supposed to rest. It's not anger. It's the brain misfiring in sleep."

Robert exhaled shakily. "So I'm not losing my mind."

"No," I said, quietly. "But we have to watch this closely. Sometimes, it can appear years before other brain conditions — like Parkinson's — but not always. For now, we keep you safe."

Sylvie nodded. "What should we do?"

"Clear the room," I told them. "Nothing sharp. Separate beds until we control it. Medication can quiet the movements."

When they stood to leave, Robert paused at the door. "Doctor," he asked softly, "if my body acts out my dreams… does that mean my dreams are dangerous?"

I looked at him — a man frightened not by what he'd seen, but by what slept inside him. "No," I said. "It means your dreams are too alive. Your body just forgot they were supposed to stay inside your head."

He nodded, eyes lowered, and reached for his wife's hand. For the first time that evening, she didn't pull away.

They walked out together — two souls learning to live where the line between sleep and waking had grown thin.

51

The Strange Accents

Her name was Janhvi — a soft-spoken schoolteacher from Kerala. She arrived with her brother, who looked both protective and unsure, as though he'd brought her to me not for treatment, but for understanding.

"What seems to be the problem?" I asked.

He hesitated. "Doctor… maybe you should talk to her yourself." Then he quietly stepped out.

Janhvi lingered in the doorway, clutching her handbag as if it might anchor her. When she finally spoke, her words were calm — but her voice was not her own.

"Doctor," she said slowly, "I am in trouble."

Her voice carried a strange rhythm — the clipped, rounded tones of northern Europe. Not her native Malayalam accent. Not even Indian English. It sounded… German.

For a moment, I wondered if I had misheard. "Were you living abroad?" I asked.

She shook her head. "No, sir. I've never left Kerala. I've never even met anyone from Germany." Then she told me about the accident.

A year earlier, on a short trip with friends, her car had flipped over. A mild head injury, a few bruises, two days in the hospital — nothing that seemed life-changing. She was back at school within a week.

And then, one morning, her mother asked, "Janhvi, why are you talking like that?"

Her colleagues noticed it next. Her students teased her. "Miss, you sound like a foreigner!" Even her brother thought she was pretending.

"Doctor," she said, her voice breaking, "everyone thinks I'm doing this on purpose — to sound fancy. But I can't stop it. I can't make my old voice come back."

I asked her to read aloud. She began — and the sound was unmistakable: the melody of another tongue woven into her English, every vowel rounded, every consonant shifted.

Then she played me a voice recording from before the crash — a school announcement, her voice bright, familiar, full of her hometown's warmth. The difference was chilling.

I leaned forward. "Janhvi," I said gently, "I think I know what's happening." Her eyes searched mine, desperate.

"What you're experiencing," I said, "is something very rare. It's called Foreign Accent Syndrome."

She froze. "You mean… this is real?"

"Yes. It's real — and it isn't your fault."

I explained that her accident likely caused a small injury in her brain — in the region that shapes how we form sounds. The words were still hers, but the music of them had changed.

Foreign Accent Syndrome (FAS) is one of the rarest neurological conditions known. It happens when tiny areas in the brain — often in the left frontal or temporal lobe — are disrupted by trauma, stroke, or disease. These regions control speech timing, pitch, and movement.

The result is an illusion. The person isn't truly speaking another accent; the subtle changes in muscle control make their normal speech sound foreign. To others, it sounds deliberate. To the speaker, it feels like being trapped in a voice that isn't theirs.

"Doctor," Janhvi whispered, "will I ever sound like me again?"

"There's hope," I said. "Speech therapy, time, and healing can help. Many people recover. Some completely."

Weeks later, her brain scan confirmed it — a small lesion in her speech-motor cortex, a scar left by the concussion. We began therapy at once.

At first, she struggled. Each session felt like wrestling a ghost — trying to summon the voice that once felt natural. She wept when she couldn't. But slowly, the rhythm returned. The accent softened. The laughter in her speech — once buried beneath the strange new tone — began to sound like home again.

Months later, she walked into my office smiling. "Doctor," she said softly, "my students say I sound like myself again."

I smiled back. "That's because you are."

"Sometimes the brain loses its compass — and the voice forgets the way home."

52

Those Who Love Filth

Her name was Susan. A retired schoolteacher from Toronto — the kind of woman parents once trusted without question. Neat handwriting, punctual lessons, strict discipline. For most of her life, order had been her religion.

But years after retirement, her neighbors began to whisper. A foul smell drifted from her house, something sour and decaying. Mice scurried under her porch. Windows stayed shut through every season. When no one dared to knock, the city finally called me.

My assistant, Dr. Derrick, came along. From the outside, Susan's home looked swallowed — vines wrapped around the porch, shrubs pressed against the windows. The front door creaked as if it hadn't been opened in years.

The air inside hit us like a wave. It was thick, wet, and rancid. The kind of smell that clings to your hair, your clothes, your skin.

We stepped into a narrow tunnel of trash — old newspapers, broken furniture, rusted tins, food wrappers. The floor was buried. We could only move sideways through the clutter. A single bulb flickered from the ceiling, buzzing faintly.

Then she appeared. Susan — thin, gray-haired, wearing a faded sweater and calm eyes that didn't match her surroundings.

"Good afternoon, Doctor," she said evenly. "I've been expecting someone from the city."

Her tone wasn't confused. It was slightly annoyed, like a woman interrupted in the middle of something important.

"Susan," I said gently, "why have you kept so many things?"

She frowned. "These aren't things, Doctor. They're useful. Every box, every paper. People throw life away too easily. I don't."

Her voice was steady, proud.

Dr. Derrick tried to explain that her neighbors were worried — about the smell, the insects, the risk of infection.

Susan gave a small laugh. "They just want my property. They've always been jealous."

It was clear what this was. Not madness — at least not the kind that shouts. This was something quieter, slower, more tragic.

Susan was living with **Diogenes Syndrome** — a rare behavioral disorder, most often seen in the elderly who live alone. It's marked by **extreme self-neglect**, **domestic squalor**, and **a compulsive hoarding of rubbish**.

Despite the name, it has nothing to do with the Greek philosopher Diogenes, who rejected wealth by choice. In this illness, the rejection of order isn't philosophical — it's pathological.

People with this condition stop noticing what most of us can't ignore. The smell. The filth. The danger. They withdraw from the world, convinced they are fine. Often, they have other medical problems — dementia, psychosis, or the slow unraveling of the mind that comes with age and isolation.

Susan's medical file told the rest: high blood pressure, signs of early dementia, untreated for years. After she retired, her routines dissolved. Her children moved away. The world became quieter, smaller. She began eating whatever she found, stopped bathing, and surrounded herself with what she could not throw away.

Her house — once a symbol of order — had become her fortress. And her prison.

Treatment was almost impossible. She refused every offer of help, locking the door against cleaning crews and city workers.

When we visited, she'd sometimes shout through the door, other times let us in for a few minutes. With patience, we earned her trust — enough to check her blood pressure, to make sure she was eating, to coax her toward therapy.

Progress came in inches. A few good days, then a retreat. One week she'd thank us. The next, she'd slam the door, accusing us of trying to steal her home.

It wasn't filth she loved. It was control — the illusion that the chaos was hers to command.

People think such cases are about dirt and decay. But really, they are about **loneliness** — about a mind folding in on itself, building walls from anything it can find.

Susan once lived to teach order to others. Now, surrounded by ruin, she clung to what little order she had left: the decision to keep everything, even the garbage.

53

The Unquenchable Lust

She was thirty-six, a schoolteacher from Ireland. Let's call her Sarah. When she entered my office, she looked hollow — eyes swollen from crying, lips trembling, her hands gripping the edge of the chair as if to keep still. For a long moment, she said nothing.

Then, in a voice that barely reached the room, she whispered, "Doctor… something has cursed me."

At first, I thought she was speaking in metaphor. But then her words spilled out — fast, tangled, desperate.

"It happens anywhere," she said. "While I'm teaching, cooking, even standing at the market. Suddenly, my body comes alive — heat, pulsing, throbbing — and I can't make it stop. It's not desire. It's not even pleasure. It's torture."

Her face burned with shame. "I went to confession," she murmured. "The priest said it was the devil testing me. But I know it isn't sin, Doctor. It's my body — it's turning against me."

What she described wasn't ordinary arousal. It came without warning, lasted for hours, sometimes days. Sex offered no relief — sometimes it made things worse.

Her husband had tried to understand, at first. But confusion turned to frustration, then silence. Love became something strained — bruised by guilt and exhaustion.

Sarah stopped going out. The vibration of a bus seat, even the hum of a washing machine, could set off another wave. She lived in quiet fear — not of the world, but of being seen in her own skin.

She had already visited several doctors. Most told her it was "just a high sex drive." Others dismissed her entirely.

But I listened. And when she finished, I said softly, "Sarah, there's a name for what you're describing."

She looked up for the first time.

"It's called Persistent Genital Arousal Disorder, or PGAD," I said. "It's real — and it's not your fault."

PGAD, sometimes called Restless Genital Syndrome, is rare — painfully so. It's a neurological and vascular condition where the body's arousal signals misfire. The person feels constant physical sensations — throbbing, pressure, heat — even without desire or thought.

It isn't lust. It's a light left on in the body, with no switch to turn it off. Medical research suggests several possible causes: compressed nerves in the pelvis or spine, varicose veins that disturb blood flow, or links to other neurological conditions like Restless Legs Syndrome. But sometimes, no cause is ever found.

The sensations are not eased by orgasm — they return, again and again, leaving the person anxious, ashamed, and exhausted.

When I told Sarah this, she began to cry again — but this time, the tears were different.

"So I'm not mad?" she asked.

"No," I said. "You're not."

Treatment is slow and complex — pelvic therapy, relaxation techniques, nerve medications, counseling for the weight of shame she'd carried alone. Her husband learned to help not by solving it, but by standing beside her. With time, the fear began to lift.

Healing didn't mean the sensations disappeared. It meant that Sarah learned they were not her fault — and that she was more than what her body had done to her.

54

The Imposter Hospital

It was a quiet afternoon in the neurology ward when I first met John Smith — a sixty-year-old school principal with a teacher's grace still written in the way he sat and spoke. His hair was silvered, his shirt perfectly pressed. But there was a strange stillness in his eyes — a kind of wonder tinged with unease.

He had suffered a stroke two months earlier. The damage was in the right frontal lobe — a part of the brain that helps us understand where we are in space, how the world fits together, what's real and what's imagined.

He spoke clearly, remembered dates and faces with precision. But there was one thing he would not believe.

"Doctor," he said softly, "this hospital isn't real."

I frowned. "What do you mean, Mr. Smith?"

He leaned in, as though letting me in on a secret. "The real hospital — Rosewood General — is near my school, in Rosewood Park. This place looks exactly like it. Every hallway, every nurse, even the smell of the floors. But this one's a copy. Someone has made a second hospital."

His daughter, standing beside him, touched his shoulder. "Papa, this IS Rosewood General. You're in Victoria. Look — even Dr. Mathew is here."

He turned to me with calm conviction. "Doctor, I know you mean well. But you don't realize it — they've copied everything. You might even be part of it without knowing."

There was no confusion about who he was. He knew his name, his family, his long years as a teacher. But something inside him — something quiet and deep — had shifted.

When I asked him how he could tell it was a copy, he smiled faintly. "I've caught children copying essays all my life," he said. "You just know when something isn't the original. The details may be perfect, but the feeling isn't."

That sentence stayed with me for weeks. At home, his daughter said, he became angry when anyone insisted it was the real hospital. He accused her of joining a conspiracy — of pretending. It broke her heart to see him that way: lucid, intelligent, but convinced the world had split in two. John Smith was living with something rare — a condition called **Reduplicative Paramnesia**.

It happens when injury to the right or frontal parts of the brain disturbs how we connect memory, emotion, and geography. The result: the mind recognizes a place but loses its anchor in reality. It believes there are two of them — one true, one false.

The person doesn't forget faces or names. They simply believe the world has been duplicated. Where Capgras Syndrome makes you doubt a person's identity, Reduplicative Paramnesia makes you doubt a place. It's as though the brain's inner compass — the invisible map that keeps us grounded — has quietly spun off course.

I told his family not to argue with him. Logic can't mend a broken map. Instead, we focused on gentle grounding — walking him through familiar details, rebuilding his sense of space, helping his brain rediscover what "real" felt like.

Months later, I found him sitting by the window, watching evening light fall across the buildings. When he turned, he smiled.

"Doctor," he said, "I've stopped fighting with everyone. Maybe you're right. Maybe I'm right too. Perhaps both hospitals exist — yours and mine. One here…" — he tapped his temple — "…and one out there."

I nodded. Because in a way, he was right. The mind, when wounded, doesn't always shatter — sometimes it builds a second world to keep the first from slipping away.

55

Exploding Head

Michael was a quiet man. The kind who spoke softly, thought carefully, and lived neatly — the sort of person whose calm steadied everyone around him. For twenty years, he had worked as a bank officer, counting numbers and balancing books. His life was ordered. Predictable. Safe.

Until the nights began to explode. He sat across from me one morning, his fingers trembling slightly. For a long while, he said nothing. Then, in a voice that carried both shame and exhaustion, he whispered — "Doctor… please don't think I'm mad."

He swallowed hard, eyes fixed on the floor. "Every night, just as I start to fall asleep, I hear it — a massive explosion inside my head. Like a gun going off. Or thunder right next to my ear. It's so real, I jump up gasping. But when I turn on the light…" He paused. "…there's nothing. My wife's asleep. The world's quiet. Only I've heard it."

Sometimes it wasn't an explosion, he said — sometimes a sharp whistle, or a door slamming in the distance. But always, it came from nowhere.

He'd even stepped outside once at two in the morning, barefoot in the cold, convinced a nearby gas main had burst. The street was silent. Only his heart was racing.

For three long months, sleep had become a threat. He feared the moment his eyes closed, afraid that the next breath would bring another invisible blast.

When he finished, I said gently, "Michael, what you're describing has a name. It's called Exploding Head Syndrome."

He blinked, startled. "That's… an actual thing?"

"Yes," I said, smiling softly. "And despite how it sounds, it's harmless."

Exploding Head Syndrome (EHS) is a type of parasomnia — a group of sleep disturbances that happen during the transition between waking and sleeping.

It feels like a loud explosion or crash coming from inside the head. But there is no real sound, and no pain.

Here's what happens:

- It strikes at the edge of sleep — when the brain is powering down.
- Instead of shutting off smoothly, a burst of activity fires in the brainstem, the part that handles sound and movement.
- The brain, startled by its own misfire, interprets that burst as a massive noise — a gunshot, thunder, an explosion.
- The person wakes in panic, heart racing, convinced something just happened.

There's no brain damage. No seizure. No danger — only fear.

I told him, "It's not madness, Michael. Your brain is just switching off unevenly — like a light that flickers before it goes dark. That flicker feels like a bang."

He gave a nervous laugh. "So… I'm not dying in my sleep?"

"No," I said. "You're just hearing your mind misfire. The quiet's playing tricks on you."

Over the next few weeks, we worked on calming his nights — steady sleep hours, less caffeine, no screens before bed. He began meditating. Breathing slowly before lying down. And little by little, the explosions faded.

When he returned a month later, there was a new softness in his voice. "Doctor," he said, smiling faintly, "I still wait for it sometimes… but the silence feels beautiful now."

Exploding Head Syndrome sounds terrifying, but it's the brain's strange reminder that even silence can be loud when the mind is restless.

56

Never Fading Images

Sameer was thirty-four — a gentle man with tired eyes and the quiet confidence of someone who lived through screens. He was a graphic designer, trained to make the world beautiful pixel by pixel. But lately, that same world had started to betray him.

When he came to see me, he smiled politely — the kind of smile people wear when they're afraid the truth might sound absurd.

"Doctor," he began, voice low, "I think my eyes are broken. Or maybe… it's my brain."

I nodded, waiting.

He took a breath. "Whenever I look at something — a coffee cup, a person's face, anything — it doesn't go away when I look somewhere else. It stays there, floating. Like a shadow that refuses to move on. I know it's not real, but I can still see it."

He hesitated, then added softly, "It's like my eyes won't stop looking, even after I've looked away."

He leaned forward, desperate for me to understand. "If I stare at a red balloon and then turn away, it follows me. It hovers in the air, half transparent, like a memory I can't erase."

There was no madness in his tone — only confusion, and the exhaustion of trying to trust his own vision.

I said quietly, "Sameer, what you're describing has a name. It's called Palinopsia."

He repeated the word, slowly. "Pa-lin-op-sia."

"It means to see again," I explained. "Your brain is replaying what your eyes just saw — like a projector that won't turn off. It's not your imagination. It's your visual system holding on too long."

He frowned slightly. "But… why would it do that?"

"There are a few reasons," I said. "Sometimes it happens with migraines, seizures, or after injury to the visual areas of the brain — the occipital lobe. Certain medications can also trigger it. In your case, I think it's linked to your migraines and the long hours you spend staring at bright light."

He let out a shaky breath. "So I'm not… losing my mind?"

I smiled. "No. Your mind's fine. It's just tired. Your brain is struggling to let go of what it's seen."

Palinopsia is the brain's echo — a rare visual disturbance where images linger or repeat even after the original object is gone.

There are two kinds:

- **Hallucinatory Palinopsia:** detailed, long-lasting images that can appear seconds or minutes after the real one. Often linked to migraines, seizures, or damage in the brain's visual areas.
- **Illusory Palinopsia:** brief, hazy afterimages or visual trails that appear when things move or light changes — usually caused by medication effects or visual system fatigue.

In both cases, the eyes are fine. The problem lies in the brain's visual memory — the part that refuses to stop seeing.

Over the next few weeks, Sameer adjusted his life. He dimmed his screens, took regular breaks, and learned to rest his eyes — and his mind. We treated his migraines, and gradually, the world began to settle.

Months later, he returned with a small, genuine smile. "The ghosts still visit sometimes," he said, "but they fade faster now. It's like my brain finally learned how to blink."

"Some memories fade from thought. Others fade from sight. The rarest ones linger in both."

57

The Faces in the Fire

Kanika wasn't the kind of person who usually sought help. She was thirty-five, a fashion designer with a calm grace — one of those people who always seemed to have life stitched together neatly. But that day, when she stepped into my office, there was a tremor behind her confidence — the look of someone being followed by something invisible.

She sat down slowly, folding her hands in her lap. "Doctor," she said, her voice barely above a whisper, "I think my mind is… seeing too much."

I waited.

"At first, I thought it was nothing," she continued. "A trick of the light. But now… everywhere I look, there are faces. On the ceiling. In the folds of my bedsheet. Even in my coffee foam."

She gave a short, nervous laugh. "Yesterday, there was an old man in my omelet. The day before, a crying monk on my bathroom tiles."

Her words might have sounded whimsical — even absurd — but the fear behind them was very real.

"At first, I'd take pictures and send them to my friends," she said softly. "They thought it was funny. They'd say I had a wild imagination. But now… it's not funny anymore. It feels like the world is alive. Like everything is staring back."

She looked at me, eyes wide, searching for reassurance. "I know those faces aren't real. But they feel real. I can't make them go away."

What Kanika was describing had a name — Pareidolia.

It's not an illness, not a hallucination. It's the mind's ancient habit of finding meaning in chaos — faces in clouds, animals in stars, saints in smoke. A survival instinct, hardwired deep within us.

I explained it gently. "Kanika, your brain is simply doing what it was designed to do. Long ago, when our ancestors saw a shape in the dark — something that might be a tiger — it was safer to believe it was real. The ones who saw faces in shadows survived. The ones who didn't… didn't."

She listened quietly, the tension in her shoulders softening.

"It's the same ability that makes artists, dreamers, and storytellers," I added. "The mind refuses to see emptiness. It insists on finding connection, even where there is none."

Pareidolia is the human tendency to see familiar shapes — specially faces — in random patterns. It's why we see:

- Eyes and mouths in car grilles or electrical outlets.
- Animals in clouds.
- Figures in burnt toast or coffee foam.
- The "Man in the Moon," or the "Face on Mars."

This happens because the brain's facial-recognition systems — especially in the temporal and occipital regions — are overactive, scanning constantly for signs of life or emotion. It's not a flaw. It's a deeply wired instinct — one that says: Better to see a face that isn't there than to miss the one that is.

Kanika wasn't losing her mind. Her brain was simply over-interpreting the world — an artist's brain working overtime.

Over the next few weeks, we focused on rest, quiet, and acceptance. When her anxiety eased, so did the faces.

One morning, months later, she returned with a lightness I hadn't seen before. "Doctor," she said, smiling, "I still see faces sometimes.

But now they don't scare me. They make me laugh. I think my brain just refuses to believe that the world is empty."

She looked toward the window, where sunlight was breaking into patterns on the wall. "It's strange," she whispered. "The moment you stop fearing the faces… they become beautiful."

58

Colours in Love with Sound

She arrived wrapped in colour. A crimson scarf, catching the light like liquid fire, trailed behind her as she walked in. "Doctor," she said, her voice calm but curious, "I think my senses have fallen in love with each other."

Her name was **Jessica**, a thirty-two-year-old artist from Havana, now living in Toronto. Her smile carried the same strange beauty she later described to me — hues and notes blending into one another, as if the air around her was painted with invisible music.

Since childhood, Jessica's world had shimmered differently. Letters glowed. Numbers had moods. Sounds had shapes.

"When people say the letter A, I see red," she said, laughing softly. "B is blue — not sky blue, but deep ocean blue. Wednesday is always grey, and Sunday smells like oranges."

She paused, looking down at her hands. "For the longest time, I thought everyone lived like this. That everyone knew Tuesday looked like seashell pink."

Only later, when she told a friend about the colours she saw in words, did she realize how different her mind was — not broken, but beautifully crossed-wired.

Jessica lives with a rare and fascinating phenomenon called **synesthesia** — a blending of the senses, where boundaries between sight, sound, taste, and touch gently dissolve.

For most people, music is something to hear. For Jessica, music is something to see. "When a violin plays," she told me, "It paints golden ribbons in the air. A piano chord turns violet — sometimes indigo, depending on how sad it feels."

Synesthesia isn't an illness or a hallucination. It's a natural variation in the way the brain connects information — a kind of neural poetry.
In synesthetes, the brain's sensory regions overlap and communicate more than usual, allowing colours to mix with sounds, and words to sparkle with taste.

Scientists have documented many forms of synesthesia:

- **Grapheme-color synesthesia**, where letters or numbers each have their own color.

- **Chromesthesia**, where sounds — like voices or instruments — evoke flashes of colour.

- **Lexical-gustatory synesthesia**, where certain words trigger taste sensations.

- **Spatial-sequence synesthesia**, where time or numbers appear as shapes in space.

It's always **involuntary** and **consistent** — if someone sees "A" as red once, it will ALWAYS be red. The brain doesn't imagine it. It perceives it.

Jessica looked out the window, thoughtful. "Sometimes I wonder," she said softly, "if other people could see what I see — would they still think the world is ordinary?"

I smiled. "Your world isn't wrong, Jessica. It's just painted differently. Most of us hear music. You SEE it."

Her face brightened — not with relief, but recognition. "So I don't have to fix it?" she asked.

"No," I said. "You have to use it."

And she did. She began to paint what she saw — music turned into color, words transformed into light. Her art became her translation of a world most of us can only imagine.

There is no cure for synesthesia — because there's nothing to cure. It's a reminder that the human mind can still make art out of its own wiring.

Before leaving, Jessica turned to me and said, almost in a whisper, "When someone says the word love, I see gold. Always gold."

That is really wonderful, I added

59

Mind That Connects Every Dot

Zara came to see me one heavy afternoon, the kind of day when even the air feels uncertain. Her husband walked beside her, his hand hovering near her elbow, as if afraid she might drift away. He looked uneasy. She looked… curious, almost amused.

"She's been noticing things," he said quietly.

Zara smiled. "Noticing? I'd call it understanding."

At first, he thought it was harmless — her new way of seeing the world. But soon, every number, every flicker of light, every passing sound seemed to whisper to her.

"Doctor," she said, eyes bright, "the number 237 — it follows me. I saw it three times today. It means something, doesn't it?"

Her voice carried a calm certainty, like someone describing a secret only she could hear. To her, the world wasn't random anymore. It was deliberate. License plates spoke in codes. The clouds outside her window formed letters only she could read. Even the sparrows on her balcony seemed to sing in warning.

But Zara wasn't seeing things that weren't there. She was *seeing too much* — drawing meaning from everything around her, as though reality itself had turned into a riddle. Her mind was a restless storyteller, unable to stop connecting the dots.

What she was experiencing is called apophenia — when the brain starts finding patterns and hidden messages in ordinary chaos.

We all do it, in small ways. We make wishes when a clock strikes 11:11. We think of someone and they call, and we call it fate. Our ancestors once depended on this — seeing signs in the weather or the flight of birds kept them alive.

But when that instinct grows too strong, it becomes a trap. The mind starts spinning stories where none exist. In Zara's world, nothing was coincidence. Every shadow, every number, every silence meant something. By nightfall, she was exhausted — her thoughts chasing meaning like waves chasing the shore, never able to rest.

I told her gently, "The brain doesn't like uncertainty. It tries to make sense of everything, even when there's nothing to solve."

For the first time, she looked unsure. Then she smiled, a little sadly. "So maybe it's not the world talking to me," she said. "Maybe it's just my mind trying too hard to listen."

With time and care, her thoughts began to soften. She learned to let the world be quiet again — not a code to crack, but something to simply live inside.

Zara's story stays with me. It reminds me how deeply we all crave meaning — how we try to turn chaos into poetry, noise into signs. But sometimes peace comes not from solving the pattern…but from letting the mystery be.

60

When the Heavens Open

It began on an ordinary night. Merin sat at her desk, surrounded by silence — just the faint ticking of a clock, the whisper of her pen on paper, and the low hum of a desk lamp spilling warm light over her notes.

She was studying the human brain. Then, without warning, hers decided to show her something she would never forget.

At first, the words on the page began to blur, letters bending and rippling like reflections on water. Then a flicker appeared — a silver shimmer in the corner of her eye, sharp and alive. Within moments, her vision filled with shifting light. Zigzag lines. Glowing waves. Circles that pulsed and danced like lightning behind her eyelids.

"The whole room was glowing," she told me later, her voice trembling between awe and fear. "Everything shimmered — the walls, my hands, even the air. It felt like the world was waking up."

She thought she was dreaming. She closed her eyes. The light only grew stronger — radiant ribbons spiraling through the dark. Her heartbeat slowed. Her body felt distant. For a fleeting instant, she wondered if she had slipped into another realm — one made not of matter, but of light.

And then, just as suddenly, the glow disappeared. What replaced it was pain. Deep, crushing, thunderous pain that seemed to split her skull from within.

That was her first **migraine aura**.

When she came to see me, Merin didn't speak like someone describing an illness. She spoke like someone describing a vision.

"Doctor," she whispered, "I think I saw something divine — a light that wasn't from this world."

I didn't correct her. "Maybe you did," I said. "The brain is a cathedral, Merin. And sometimes, when its walls tremble, its stained glass burns with colours no one else can see."

Medically, what she experienced was a **migraine aura** — a temporary wave of neurological activity that ripples across the brain just before the pain begins. It's not imagination, and it's not madness. It's the brain itself lighting up.

The most common aura is **visual** — flickering lights, zigzag lines, blind spots that grow and shift like living things. Some see them as shining fortresses or prisms breaking apart. Others experience **sensory auras** — tingling that travels from the fingertips up the arm, sometimes touching the lips or tongue. A few feel **language auras** — words slipping away, speech tangled in fog.

These episodes usually last between five and sixty minutes, caused by a wave of electrical change called **cortical spreading depression**, which moves across the brain's surface. Not everyone with migraines experiences auras, but for those who do, they can feel like both a warning and a visitation.

A young boy once told me, "Doctor, before my headache comes, I see a palace made of light. It hums like music."

Science calls it a neurological event. But when you listen to the way people describe it — the beauty, the terror, the stillness — you begin to wonder if it's also something more.

Merin no longer fears the light that comes before the pain.

"It hurts," she said quietly, "but it's also… beautiful. For a moment, I see something vast. It feels like heaven opened — just enough for me to look in."

61

The Magical City

The city of Jerusalme lies bathed in gold — domes gleaming, alleys still hushed, a slow wind whispering through olive trees. Somewhere, a muezzin's call rises and fades, and the bells of a nearby monastery answer in kind.

That's when the call came.

"Doctor," my secretary said, "they've brought in a man from the Leonardo Plaza Hotel. He's wrapped in bedsheets and says he's a prophet."

By the time I reached the office, the morning light was just beginning to touch the blinds.

Daniel sat quietly, a white sheet draped across his shoulders like a robe. His wife beside him — pale, anxious, fingers trembling.

"He's never been like this," she said quickly. "He's a teacher. Rational. He believes in God, yes, but he's not… extreme. This trip was meant to be beautiful."

Daniel looked up at me. His expression was calm — luminous, even. He held a rolled towel in his hand as if it were a sacred scroll.

"I am a prophet," he said softly. "The Lord spoke to me. He told me the time has come. I've been chosen to warn the world."

I asked gently, "When did this begin, Daniel?"

His eyes flickered, distant. "Last night," he said. "I was walking near the Western Wall. The stones began to glow. Then they spoke. Each one said: You are the messenger. Their voices grew until they filled me. I am Elijah returned."

He looked at me, pleading and certain. "You believe me, don't you?"

I smiled faintly. "Perhaps. Though I never imagined Elijah arriving in a hotel bedsheet."

He didn't smile back. "If I don't speak, the world will fall into darkness," he murmured. "They're waiting for me, Doctor. In the square. I must go."

His voice was gentle, but his conviction unbreakable — the kind that cannot be reasoned with, only witnessed.

Daniel was not delusional in the usual sense. His words were coherent, his eyes steady. What had seized him was something far older, deeper — something that breathes beneath the stones of that city.

Jerusalem has that power. It is a place where history and faith share the same air, where prayers from a thousand years still echo between walls. For some, it is holy ground. For others, it becomes a mirror that shows too much.

Daniel suffered from **Jerusalem Syndrome** — a rare psychological condition that can overwhelm ordinary people visiting the Holy City.

It begins suddenly: A surge of religious fervor. A need for purity — washing, cleansing, dressing in white. **It unfolds quietly.** The person withdraws. Begins preaching. Believes they have been chosen by God. **And it ends just as suddenly:** When removed from the city's charged atmosphere, the voices fade. Reality returns.

Daniel's did too.

A few days after leaving Jerusalem, he was himself again — confused, apologetic, unable to explain what had taken hold of him. The prophet's robe became a sheet once more. The scroll, a towel. The light, only morning sun.

Still, I remember the look in his eyes that day — the kind of faith that borders on fire. Because for a heartbeat in time, the city had whispered —and Daniel had listened.

62

The Green-Eyed Professor

He was a man known for his mind. A scientist, mid-forties — sharp, disciplined, the kind of person who trusted reason above all else. The hospital director had called me himself. "Please see him," he said. "He's losing sleep — and something more."

When Professor Ken entered my office, he looked hollow. The kind of tired that doesn't come from work but from watching one's own thoughts turn against them. His wife followed a step behind — pale, fragile, her eyes full of fear and love both.

He didn't greet me. He went straight to his truth.

"Doctor, she lies to me all the time." His voice shook with certainty. "When I'm away, she meets someone else. She says she's at the market, or the library, but I know. I know. Don't let her fool you too."

I turned to his wife. She spoke softly, as though afraid her words might break him. "I've never betrayed him," she whispered. "But he doesn't believe me anymore. He checks my calls, follows me to work, even questions the children. I can't convince him of anything."

Professor Ken reached into his bag and placed a worn notebook on my desk. "Here," he said. "My evidence."

Each page was filled with timestamps, sketches, fragments — small details collected like data points in an endless experiment. Her footsteps, sighs, a stranger's passing glance. To him, every mark was proof.

As I listened, I realized I was not speaking to a jealous man. I was speaking to a mind caught in its own trap — intelligent, methodical, and absolutely certain.

He was suffering from **Othello Syndrome** — a rare and haunting psychiatric condition named after Shakespeare's tragic hero. It is not ordinary jealousy. It is delusion — an unshakable belief that one's partner is unfaithful, no matter the truth, no matter the evidence to the contrary.

In this disorder, the mind twists every act of love into suspicion. A late reply becomes a confession. A moment of silence becomes deceit. And every attempt at reassurance only feeds the fire.

Othello Syndrome can appear in people struggling with other illnesses — schizophrenia, dementia, even after certain brain injuries or with substance abuse. It is one of the most dangerous forms of delusion, not because it begins violently, but because it almost always ends that way.

"Professor," I said quietly, "is it possible that your mind — so used to solving — might be creating patterns that aren't there?"

He looked at me for a long moment. "Doctor," he said coldly, "you don't understand. She's clever. You've already taken her side."

His wife wept silently. He did not look at her. His eyes were fixed on a world only he could see — a world where betrayal was constant and truth no longer existed.

Othello Syndrome is cruel. It eats away at trust until love itself begins to rot. No proof of innocence can cure it, because the disease doesn't live in logic — it lives in fear. And fear, once it learns to disguise itself as certainty, never truly sleeps.

63

When the Stars Fall in Love

It happened in a time of shadows and mourning. Rajiv Gandhi was Prime Minister then. The air in Delhi still carried the ache of Indira's death. Around the Prime Minister's home, soldiers stood like statues — alert, unmoving, guarding the gates of power and grief.

One warm afternoon, a man appeared outside those gates. Young. Ordinary. His clothes neat, his manner calm — except for the strange light in his eyes. He told the guards he had come for **Priyanka Gandhi**.

"She loves me," he said softly. "But her father wouldn't understand. She sends me messages through the television. Every time she smiles, it's for me."

He tried to walk past the barricades to "free" her from her silence. The guards stopped him before he could cross. He didn't fight. He simply looked up at the sky and whispered, "You can't stop love from finding its way."

Later, when questioned, he spoke gently, almost tenderly — as though sharing a secret too beautiful to doubt. "She'll reach me again," he said. "You'll see."

He wasn't a fanatic. He wasn't violent. He was certain. And his story wasn't unique.

Across the world, I've seen others like him — drawn by the same invisible thread. A man waiting outside a concert hall, convinced a singer loves him. A woman writing letters to an actor she's never met, believing every line of his script is meant for her. Princess Diana. Aishwarya Rai. Ustad Zakir Hussain. Each has had strangers who lived entirely within a love story that only one heart believed in.

The condition has a name. **Erotomania.** A rare delusional disorder where a person becomes convinced that someone — often a celebrity or figure of power — is secretly in love with them. It starts innocently, like admiration. A smile, a lyric, a passing glance. Then, slowly, reality begins to shift.

A look on television becomes a signal, line in a speech becomes a message. A silence becomes proof of love, hidden by circumstance.

They wait. They write. They listen for signs. And when the object of their affection denies it, they smile again because to them, that denial is only part of the secret language lovers share.

Medically, Erotomania is well-defined. It belongs to a group of **delusional disorders**, in which belief overrides all evidence. The person is absolutely certain that the love exists — unshaken by logic or proof to the contrary.

Often, Erotomania coexists with other psychiatric conditions — such as schizophrenia, bipolar disorder, or substance-induced psychosis. But at its heart, it is something both fragile and tragic: a mind so desperate to be loved that it creates the proof itself.

Researchers at Princeton once described it as "a love that exists only in one mind, yet feels as real as breath."

That's what makes it haunting. It isn't deception. It's devotion — miswired. A story the brain tells itself when loneliness grows louder than truth. To those who suffer it, love is not a choice. It's a voice. And that voice, no matter how far away, keeps calling their name.

64

Getting Drunk Without Alcohol

It began like most mistakes do — with flashing lights. The siren tore through the dark, painting the empty road in red and blue. Evan Smith blinked hard, the world tilting around him as his car slowed to a stop.

"Step out of the vehicle," the officer said.

Evan's hands shook as he opened the door. The air felt heavy, unreal.
He hadn't had a drink. He knew that. But his legs didn't agree. The officer held up the breathalyzer. It beeped.

0.18%. Twice the legal limit.

The officer sighed. "You've had a good night, huh?"

Evan's voice cracked. "I swear, officer… I haven't had a drink."

The man smirked. "Sure. And I'm the Pope." The cuffs clicked shut.

By morning, his name was everywhere. **"Social Worker Arrested for Drunk Driving."**

Evan Smith — the quiet man who helped broken families — was now branded a liar, a drunk. His wife sat beside him in court, her eyes red, her hands trembling.

"He doesn't drink," she said softly. "Not a drop. But sometimes… it's like something inside him changes. He stumbles. Slurs. Then it's gone."

The judge rubbed his forehead. "We'll have a full medical evaluation."

Evan leaned forward, voice barely a whisper. "No one's going to believe me."

When I met him, he looked hollow — like someone who'd spent months defending a crime he couldn't even understand.

"Doctor," he said quietly, "I lose control. My head spins. My body feels drunk. But I haven't touched alcohol. Please… tell me I'm not crazy."

He wasn't lying. I could tell. We admitted him under observation. No alcohol. No visitors. Every meal measured, recorded, and logged.

He ate rice, bread, fruit. Ordinary food. A few hours later, a nurse rushed in, her face pale. "Doctor," she said, "his blood alcohol is rising."

I stared at the chart. It was impossible — and yet there it was. His body was brewing alcohol. Inside him, yeast and bacteria were feasting on sugar, turning it into ethanol — the same chemical that makes us drunk. His stomach had become a distillery. His gut, a ghostly brewery working without consent.

Days later, I stood in court. The air was still. The judge leaned forward.

"Doctor," he said, "you're telling us this man became intoxicated… without drinking?"

"Yes, Your Honor," I replied. "He suffers from Auto-Brewery Syndrome."

A murmur rippled through the room.

"It's rare," I continued. "In some people, microorganisms in the gut ferment carbohydrates into alcohol. Mr. Smith's blood alcohol levels rose naturally. His body turned food into liquor."

The judge sat back, silent. "So he wasn't drunk by choice," he said quietly.

"No," I said. "He was drunk by biology."

Evan was acquitted. His name cleared. But vindication doesn't heal everything. When I saw him months later, he was thinner, quieter. The weight of disbelief still clung to him.

He smiled faintly. "You saved my life, Doc. I thought I was losing my mind. Turns out, it was just my stomach brewing beer behind my back." He laughed softly, almost bitterly. "Imagine being drunk… on your own body."

I smiled. "Sometimes," I said, "the cruelest battles are the ones that happen inside us."

Auto-Brewery Syndrome

In rare cases, yeast or bacteria living in the gut begin to ferment carbohydrates into alcohol. The result: intoxication — without ever touching a drink.

Symptoms include slurred speech, dizziness, fatigue, and blackouts. Because the body produces the alcohol internally, breath tests and blood reports can mimic that of a heavy drinker.

The condition is often caused by gut dysbiosis — an imbalance in intestinal microbes, sometimes triggered by antibiotics or high-carbohydrate diets.

Treatment involves antifungal therapy, probiotics, and strict dietary control.
Recovery is possible — but the misunderstanding can ruin lives long before healing begins.

Evan's case reminded us of something medicine too often forgets: sometimes, what looks like guilt is just a body misfiring in the dark.

65

Monster's Hunger

The snow came early that year — thick, endless, and silent. It covered the pines, buried the trails, and sealed the little village in white. In that kind of winter, sound travels differently. Every creak of the wood, every whisper of wind, feels alive.

That's when I first heard about **Nodin**. He was a man of thirty — quiet, strong, a hunter who lived by the rhythm of the seasons. The elders respected him. He worked hard, kept to himself, and never wasted a word. But that winter, something inside him began to unravel.

He stopped eating. At first, they thought it was just the hunger everyone was feeling — the meat frozen, the stores running low. But Nodin's wife noticed he refused food even when it was placed before him. He said the smell of meat made him sick. Then came the nightmares.

He woke drenched in sweat, trembling, saying he saw eyes in the dark. Not animal eyes — human ones, staring from the forest.

Soon, he stopped sleeping at all. He whispered that something was inside him — something ancient, cold, and hungry. His friends laughed it off, until one night he called them to his cabin.

They found him sitting by the fire, his face hollow, his voice barely human.
"You know the stories," he said. "The WENDIGO — the creature that eats flesh when winter takes away everything else." They nodded. It was an old legend, meant to scare children away from greed and cannibalism.

But Nodin's next words chilled the room. "It's in me," he whispered. "That hunger. I feel it crawling under my skin. I dream of tearing flesh. I don't want to — but I can't stop the thought. Please… keep away from me."

His friends stared in horror. They prayed. They burned sage. They sang the old songs to drive away spirits. But the fear didn't leave him — it grew stronger.

The next morning, Nodin locked himself inside his hut. For three days, no one saw him. When they finally forced the door open, he was lying on the floor — alive, but barely. His eyes were wild, his lips cracked from thirst. He whispered, "The hunger is gone… but it took something from me."

They brought him to our hospital. He was weak, trembling, and spoke in short, broken sentences. As I examined him, I realized this wasn't a story of demons or folklore. This was something darker — and human.

Wendigo Psychosis — a rare psychiatric condition once described among Indigenous communities in North American tribe mainly Algonquin. It begins with deep anxiety and isolation — often during harsh winters when food is scarce. The person becomes obsessed with the fear of turning into a cannibal, or believes they already have.
They feel a monstrous hunger inside them — one that repulses and terrifies them at once.

It's a form of culture-bound delusion, shaped by ancestral stories that once kept people safe from desperation's worst edge. In other words, the legend that warned against inhuman hunger… became the very shape of fear itself.

Nodin stayed with us for weeks. Through therapy, warmth, and quiet reassurance, his nightmares faded. He began to eat again — little by little. Sometimes, he'd still wake up in the night, whispering, "It's watching me." But with time, the voice inside him grew quiet.

When he was ready to leave, he thanked me with tears in his eyes. "I thought the monster was real," he said softly. "But it was only the cold inside my mind."

I watched him walk out into the snow — smaller, perhaps, but freer. And for a moment, I thought I saw something move among the trees. Maybe just the wind. Or maybe the old hunger, retreating back into legend.

66

The Weird Answers

The night was slow and heavy, the kind that hums with unease. They brought him in just before the shift changed — a man in his forties, handcuffed, silent, trembling like someone half-awake from a bad dream.

His name was **Rojen**. The guards said he'd stopped making sense. "He's quiet," one of them told me. "Polite. But his answers—they're… wrong."

When I entered the small concrete cell, he was sitting on the edge of the cot, staring at the floor. The light flickered above him, carving long shadows across his face.

"Rojen," I said softly, "do you know what day it is today?"

He looked up, eyes glassy but calm. After a long pause, he said, "Blue."

I waited. "And how many fingers am I holding up?"

He studied my hand carefully, almost scientifically, then whispered, "Two hundred… maybe."

There was no defiance in his tone. No mockery. Only confusion — deep, unshakable, and strangely innocent.

He glanced around the room. "Doctor, this isn't a prison, right?" he murmured.
"It looks like my old school… but everyone's wearing the same clothes."

His words trembled as if pulled from a dream he couldn't quite escape. For a moment, fear flickered through his face — not the fear of punishment, but the fear of losing the map to his own mind.

This was **Ganser Syndrome** — one of psychiatry's rarest ghosts. A state where the mind drifts between knowing and not knowing, reality and illusion.

People with it give **approximate answers** to simple questions — close, but not quite right. Ask them the color of blood, they might say green. Ask the time, they'll tell you Tuesday. It's often seen in those who've reached the breaking point — **prisoners, soldiers, people who have stared too long into despair.** The brain, overwhelmed by fear or guilt, takes a strange escape route. It doesn't forget — it misfires. It starts to speak in riddles, as if protecting itself from truths too sharp to face.

Some call it malingering — faking madness. But I've looked into the eyes of men like Rojen, and I know: no actor could hold that kind of lostness.

When I left that night, he was still whispering numbers under his breath, trying to make sense of the world by counting it. Somewhere behind those fractured words, I could feel him searching — for one answer that would finally make sense again.

In the corridor, the guards looked at me for explanation. I only said, "His mind isn't lying. It's hiding."

"Between sense and nonsense lies a thin line of mercy where the mind retreats to protect what's left of itself."

67

The Night Visitor

(Excerpt from a lecture by Dr. Bradley, Neurology Department, University of Toronto Teaching Hospital)

Dr. Bradley: Let me tell you about a girl named **Limiya.** She was fourteen — from a small coastal town called Nicaguruu. A quiet child, graceful in that unspoken way some lives carry light even when surrounded by shadow.

When her file first reached my desk, it seemed ordinary — no history of illness, no injury, no sign of delusion. But one line made me stop.

"WAKES UP UNABLE TO MOVE. CLAIMS TO SEE A DARK FIGURE WATCHING HER." Her mother described it with trembling words:

"IT'S LIKE THE NIGHT ITSELF IS SITTING ON HER CHEST."

When I first met Limiya, she sat very still on the examination table, hands folded in her lap. There was something about her eyes — wide, sleepless, haunted. Her voice barely reached me when she began to speak.

"It starts when I wake up," she said. "I can see everything — my room, the curtain, the light on the wall. But I can't move. I can't even scream. I feel something close… like it's waiting for me."

So I asked her, "What do you see?"

She hesitated, then whispered,

"Sometimes it's a shadow. Sometimes I feel it sit beside me. Once, it leaned close — as if it wanted to whisper my name."

Now, class — understand this. The fear she felt was real, even if the visitor was not. What she was experiencing had a name: **Sleep Paralysis** — one of the strangest intersections between the waking and dreaming worlds.

It's what happens when the mind wakes up before the body does. Normally, during **REM sleep**, your brain keeps your body still through a state called **atonia** — a kind of natural paralysis that keeps you from acting out your dreams. But sometimes, that switch misfires. The brain wakes too early, while the body remains frozen.

For those few seconds — or minutes — you're caught between two realities. You're awake, but your body won't obey you. Your room is the same, but it doesn't feel safe anymore. The air thickens. The heartbeat echoes. Every sound becomes a whisper from the dark.

Many people see things — shadows, intruders, faces — what we call **hypnopompic hallucinations**. Others feel a crushing weight on their chest, known as the **incubus phenomenon,** the brain's way of translating panic into touch.

It's not possession. It's not madness. It's the body's rhythm gone momentarily astray — a fragile confusion between sleep and wakefulness. Common triggers? Fatigue. Irregular sleep. Stress. Sometimes, simply sleeping on your back.

We treated Limiya gently—adjusted her sleep schedule, encouraged her to rest on her side, taught her to breathe through the paralysis instead of fighting it. Slowly, the nights began to lose their teeth.

Weeks later, she sent me a letter. "I still feel it sometimes, Doctor," she wrote, "but now, I just wait. And it goes away."

I keep that letter in my drawer — not because it's rare, but because it reminds me how thin the line is between the real and the imagined. And how fear, when given a heartbeat, can feel as real as life itself.

So, when someone tells you they've woken to shadows pressing on their chest — don't laugh, and don't dismiss it. Just listen. Because sometimes, what they're describing… is the place where dreams forget to end.

*****

Bibliography

I. Foundational Texts in Psychiatry and Psychology

American Psychiatric Association. (2022). Diagnostic and Statistical Manual of Mental Disorders (5th ed., Text Revision). Washington, DC: American Psychiatric Publishing.

Kaplan, H. I., & Sadock, B. J. (2015). Comprehensive Textbook of Psychiatry (10th ed.). Wolters Kluwer.

Sims, A. (2018). Symptoms in the Mind: An Introduction to Descriptive Psychopathology (5th ed.). Saunders.

Jaspers, K. (1997). General Psychopathology (Trans. J. Hoenig & M. W. Hamilton). Johns Hopkins University Press. (Original work published 1913)

Nolen-Hoeksema, S. (2014). Abnormal Psychology (7th ed.). McGraw-Hill Education.

II. Rare and Unusual Psychiatric Syndromes

Enoch, D., & Trethowan, W. (1991). Uncommon Psychiatric Syndromes (4th ed.). CRC Press.

Blom, J. D. (2010). A Dictionary of Hallucinations. Springer.

Oyebode, F. (2015). Mindreadings: Introductory Selections on Clinical Psychiatry. RCPsych Publications.

Hacking, I. (1998). Mad Travelers: Reflections on the Reality of Transient Mental Illnesses. Harvard University Press.

Berrios, G. E., & Luque, R. (1995). Cotard's Syndrome: Analysis of 100 Cases. Acta Psychiatrica Scandinavica, 91(3), 185–188.

III. Neurological and Neuropsychiatric Sources

Ramachandran, V. S., & Blakeslee, S. (1998). Phantoms in the Brain: Probing the Mysteries of the Human Mind. HarperCollins.

Sacks, O. (1985). The Man Who Mistook His Wife for a Hat. Summit Books.

Geschwind, N., & Kaplan, E. (1962). A Human Behavioral Syndrome Associated with Temporal Lobe Lesions. Brain, 85(3), 573–587.

Trimble, M. R. (2007). The Soul in the Brain: The Cerebral Basis of Language, Art, and BELIEF. Johns Hopkins University Press.

Bear, D. M., & Fedio, P. (1977). Quantitative Analysis of Interictal Behavior in Temporal Lobe Epilepsy. Archives of Neurology, 34(8), 454–467.

IV. Cultural and Cross-Cultural Psychiatry

Kleinman, A. (1980). Patients and Healers in the Context of Culture. University of California Press.

Lee, S., & Kleinman, A. (2007). Are Somatoform Disorders Changing with Time? Psychosomatic Medicine, 69(9), 846–849.

Lin, K. M. (1983). Hwa-Byung: A Korean Culture-Bound Syndrome? American Journal of Psychiatry, 140(1), 105–107.

Simons, R. C., & Hughes, C. C. (1985). The Culture-Bound Syndromes: Folk Illnesses of Psychiatric and Anthropological Interest. D. Reidel Publishing.

Tseng, W. S. (2006). From Peculiar Psychiatric Disorders through Culture-Bound Syndromes to Culturally Sensitive Psychiatry. Transcultural Psychiatry, 43(4), 554–576.

V. Epilepsy, Dissociation, and the Borderlands of Psychiatry

Devinsky, O., & Schachter, S. C. (2009). Behavioral Neurology of Epilepsy. Oxford University Press.

Devinsky, O. (2003). Psychiatric Comorbidities in Epilepsy: Insights from Temporal Lobe Epilepsy. Epilepsia, 44(Suppl 4), 21–25.

Fenwick, P., & Schatz, R. (2000). The Hidden Door: Understanding Dissociation and EPILEPSY. Routledge.

Trimble, M. R. (1991). Epilepsy, Behaviour and Cognitive Function. Wiley.

VI. Narrative and Humanistic Psychiatry

Frank, A. W. (1995). The Wounded Storyteller: Body, Illness, and Ethics. University of Chicago Press.

Charon, R. (2006). Narrative Medicine: Honoring the Stories of Illness. Oxford University Press.

Yalom, I. D. (1989). Love's Executioner and Other Tales of Psychotherapy. Basic Books.

May, R. (1975). The Courage to Create. W. W. Norton & Company.

Laing, R. D. (1960). The Divided Self: An Existential Study in Sanity and Madness. Penguin Books.

VII. Historical and Philosophical Context

Foucault, M. (1961). Madness and Civilization: A History of Insanity in the Age of Reason. Vintage.

Scull, A. (2015). Madness in Civilization: A Cultural History of Insanity. Princeton University Press.

Porter, R. (2002). Madness: A Brief History. Oxford University Press.

Shorter, E. (1997). A History of Psychiatry: From the Era of the Asylum to the Age of Prozac. Wiley.

VIII. Recent Neuroscience and Consciousness Studies

Damasio, A. (1999). The Feeling of What Happens: Body and Emotion in the Making of Consciousness. Harcourt Brace.

Koch, C. (2018). The Feeling of Life Itself: Why Consciousness Is Widespread but Can't Be Computed. MIT Press.

Eagleman, D. (2011). Incognito: The Secret Lives of the Brain. Pantheon.

Seth, A. (2021). Being You: A New Science of Consciousness. Faber & Faber.

IX. Case Literature and Clinical Curiosities

Blom, J. D., & Sommer, I. E. C. (2012). Hallucinations: Research and Practice. Springer.

Trimble, M. R., & Freeman, A. (2006). Psychiatric and Behavioural Disorders in Epilepsy. Cambridge University Press.

O'Sullivan, M. (2015). Is It Me or My Brain? Understanding Functional Neurological Disorders. Yale University Press.

X. Suggested Reading for Narrative Inspiration

Sacks, O. (2019). Everything in Its Place: First Loves and Last Tales. Alfred A. Knopf.

Alexander, E. (2012). Proof of Heaven: A Neurosurgeon's Journey into the Afterlife. Simon & Schuster.

Doidge, N. (2007). The Brain That Changes Itself. Viking.

Ramachandran, V. S. (2011). The Tell-Tale Brain: A Neuroscientist's Quest for What Makes Us Human. W. W. Norton.

*****

ABOUT THE AUTHOR

Dr. Robin K. Mathew

Dr. Robin K. Mathew is a highly accomplished behavioral psychologist and ethnographer whose expertise is underpinned by extensive, global professional experience and cross-cultural engagement. His career reflects a deep appreciation for the complex socio-economic, ethnic, and linguistic variances shaping human experience, gained through direct interaction with individuals from nearly **90 different nationalities**.

Dr. Mathew possesses a diverse and distinguished professional history, holding roles such as **Research Assistant, Research Associate, Researcher, and Adjunct Faculty, Bheavioural Psychologist, Ethnographer** in prestigious international organizations. His multidisciplinary background includes formal education and experience in **Information Technology, Human Resource Management, Psychology, Cyber Forensics, and Cyber Psychology.**

He has contributed his expertise across various esteemed institutions, including the **University of Toronto, Michigan University, the Indian Institute of Management (IIM), ICFAI Business School, Best Buy, the Royal Bank of Canada, and Thomson Reuters**. These roles have cultivated an unparalleled ability to synthesize insights across disciplines, significantly enriching his psychological analyses.

Over the past twelve years, Dr. Mathew has authored and published **20 books** that delve deeply into facets of psychology and the human condition. Furthermore, he has contributed nearly **600 articles** across a wide range of subjects, published in prestigious magazines both domestically and internationally. His prolific output captures the intricate nuances of human nature, informed by the vast knowledge accumulated throughout his professional journey.

Dr. Mathew is a **Social Psychology Scientist** currently working independently as an analyst for an international media agency.

Other books by the Author:

Malayalam

1. Madamballiyille Manorogikal
2. Chekuthante Panipura
3. Chanakyante Kamukimar
4. Digital Nagavallimar
5. Cyber Parakaya Pravesham
6. Oru Kanyakayude Suvishesham
7. Jeevitha Vijyathinte Krithrima Thakkol
8. Kaanan Desham Thedi Poyavar
9. Geethanjali Voice
10. Raktham Viyarkkunna Kaikal

English

1. Lovers of Chanakya
2. In Quest of the Promised Land
3. I am Akira
4. The Expedition of Nun
5. The Artificial Key to Success
6. The Psychology of Mind Deception
7. Human Algorithm-Cyber Psychology for the Digital Age
8. The Grand Palace of Lucifer
9. The Saga of Nylari

Email: robinkmathew@gmail.com